Delivering the Customer Experience

Creating attainable dreams

A guide for retail teams

For the retailers who have inspired me, for my parents who always motivated me, for my wife Wendy, daughter Caitlin and sons Sean, Michael and Liam, for all of whom shopping is both a pleasure and an art form!

Delivering the Customer Experience

Creating attainable dreams

A guide for retail teams

Dr Mark F. Dorgan

EUROPEAN EDITION

A CIP catalogue record for this book is available at The British Library

ISBN-13: 978-0-9566904-0-1

Published by:

Dr Mark F. Dorgan, Multiplier,

139 Park Road, Teddington TW11 0BS, United Kingdom

mark_dorgan@hotmail.com

Introduction: Delivering a great customer experience

Imagine visiting a village market in the Mediterranean. You feel great because you have the warm sunshine on your cheek. The sky and the sea are bluer than you remember. Piles of brightly coloured fruit and lush vegetables invite you to touch, feel and explore. You can smell the fresh fertility of the earth and the produce. Each passageway suggests something exciting is just round that next corner.

The sights and sounds draw you in, along with the lazily milling crowd of other people similarly enjoying the market. You speak to people more easily as you drop your guard. You know that somewhere in the market there will be a vendor who is a bit of a character, inviting you to try the produce, engaging with you and others around you in light-hearted banter. You feel good. This is the life. If only…

You move on to the stalls selling honey and nuts, then leather goods – you breath in the rich smell of newly worked leather.

Whether it is this sort of experience that attracts you or another, depending on your personal preferences, what we all have in common is the desire to experience attainable dreams – the things that make up our aspirational lifestyle. We like the feelings these experiences evoke. We react emotionally with a sense of well-being. We begin to dream and plan how our lives might be transformed by engaging more deeply in the lifestyle evoked by these experiences. This could be in a very small way, as when a lemon-flavoured sweet briefly makes me think of the sweet lemons of Corsica, or in a more fundamental way, as when a great new outfit makes me feel as if I am living my aspirational dream.

By contrast, imagine the experience I had recently in a department store clothing department. After wandering the aisles looking for men's coats for some time, without being able to spot any navigation aids to help me, I looked for a member of staff. There were not many staff about, but most were leaning disconsolately on counters or chatting.

When I approached a pair of staff members, they continued chatting as if I were invisible. I had to intervene to get help. The young lady who assisted me took me to a rack of clothing that was filled with a mixture of garments in different sizes and styles, with no obvious logic.

I gave my size, upon which she said, "We don't have any in that size – you may want to try one of our other stores," and promptly walked away. Sound familiar? Needless to say, I did not try one of their other stores, but went to a retailer that provided a positive shopping experience to buy my coat.

A very powerful feature of the positive experiences is that they are best when shared with others, whether a partner or friends or, and this is a satisfying discovery, making new friends through the shared experience. This is how communities are formed – people organically grouping together and interacting based on shared experiences or interests that define a common, aspirational lifestyle. This is seen today also in the social networks that are constantly forming and reforming on-line.

And this social dimension is the heart of why people enjoy good shopping experiences. It is, I suggest, the single most important insight for any retailer, if they are to succeed. This is often strongest in younger shoppers who are exploring affiliations that will shape their lives and identities, and in women, who seem to have a stronger talent than men for creating and experiencing social communities in day-to-day life, though men are by no means exempt from this tendency.

This is what makes the customers of *Borders* USA book chain excited when they attend the book club readings with like-minded readers, to listen to their favourite author reading from his book. It is what makes them look forward to the *Twitter* messages and e-mail alerts of new developments in their chosen genre. It is what makes them visit the web-site and blogs to network with *Borders*' staff and other readers.

This is also why the customers of Mexican women's fashion chain *El Palacio de Hierro* flock to the stores and eagerly await the clever adverts, as the company has perfectly captured the spirit of "being a woman", transmitting a sense of belonging to a special group and using clever humour to highlight the unique strengths and challenges of being a woman. And so on.

There are many wonderful examples of great retailers getting it right – *Tesco*, *Apple*, *The Body Shop, Disney* and many more. We will explore a number of these during the book to illustrate the various principles and aspects of delivering a great customer experience.

This book is about how to deliver a great customer experience, so that you can create a successful retail business or transform an existing one. It will focus first on listening to customers, engaging them in a meaningful conversation and delivering the lifestyle experiences that make them come back again and again to spend their money in your store, whether a bricks and mortar, on-line or multi-channel store.

This is not just a superficial look at the cosmetic experience itself, but a systematic exploration of the research, analysis, design and delivery of well-crafted and effective customer experiences that consistently succeed, together with the concepts and tools that support these.

We will then spend some time on the 2 key enablers of delivering a great customer experience – your people and technology. In order to establish and sustain the customer experiences that will define your business in the hearts and minds of your customers, you will need motivated people who live the business ideal, who identify with the customers' aspirations and who are passionate about what they do. You will also need very specific IT tools, as this creates the opportunity for engaging with the customer in multiple channels – an essential in today's world.

Finally, I will discuss the value proposition – the importance of the right product at the right price in order to create sustainable value. This is the object of the experience, after all – to package and embody a value proposition for the customer.

I will not focus on the technical basics of retailing very formally, but rather assume that you understand the fundamental importance of having a good product, pricing and promoting it correctly, and selling it in the right locations. When I do refer to these aspects, it will be in terms of how you might use them in a more targeted way to best deliver the customer experience. My focus will remain sharply on those factors that create retailing success through customer insights, customer engagement and delivering the best customer experience in your category of retailing. Throughout the book I will refer to best practice retail examples to illustrate.

The two diagrams below will help you to navigate this book:

- The first is a pyramid showing the six building blocks of a successful retail business – the 3 pillars, the 2 enablers and the value proposition.
- The second diagram shows these same elements in a different way in the core of the diagram, adding in the outer circle all the factors we will explore through the text in Section 1. These should form a checklist and aide memoire for you in applying these principles in your work.

Diagram 1: The building blocks for sustainably delivering a great customer experience

Diagram 2: All the levers for delivering a great customer experience

I trust you will enjoy the book and the examples given and, above all, that you will find it useful and practical in transforming your performance through delivering a great customer experience.

Section 1: The 3 pillars of customer experience

Delivering the customer experience successfully, and profitably, depends on doing three things well – understanding the customers' motivations, engaging your target consumer community in a way that is meaningful to them and delivering attainable lifestyle dreams that are based on their aspirations.

A few years ago I had the pleasure of staying in the *Ritz Carlton* hotel in Sydney, Australia. In addition to a wonderful stay that perfectly met my business traveller needs, the hotel and its staff made me feel as if I was in a comfortable family hotel with their personal touch and attention to detail.

However, the experience that really made me take notice was when the Concierge approached me on my second last day there and said, "I notice you have a return flight booked to Cairns – would you like me to look after any of your luggage while you visit the Great Barrier Reef?"

The *Ritz Carlton* understood my needs, engaged with me in ways that perfectly matched both my needs and my aspirational lifestyle dreams – and then went a step further by using their insight to make my travel easier. They didn't have to do that, as I would still have gone on my way with a positive view of their hotel, but that final touch has ensured I will always stay in their hotel when I am in Sydney.

In the retail sector, the French group *Carrefour* demonstrated that it understood the customers' motivations, engaged its target consumer community in a way that is meaningful to them and delivered attainable lifestyle dreams that are based on their aspirations when it pioneered the modern hypermarket format in 1963. This delivered all the freshness and convenience of a traditional market in a modern environment that met consumers' needs, with the convenience of plenty of parking and low prices. Faithfully replicating this winning formula in different regions and countries around the world has allowed *Carrefour* to become one of the few truly global retailers, the second biggest in the world after *Walmart.*

In this section we will explore the ideas, methods and some best practice cases for understanding and engaging with your customers, as well as delivering the attainable dreams – this is the heart of this book.

Diagram 3: The 3 pillars of customer experience

You may have a great product, great people and the technology to support your business, but if you do not truly understand and engage with your target customers, delivering a great customer experience, you do not have a viable retail business.

So how do we do this?

The 1st pillar: Understand customer motivation

Understanding consumer motivation has always been important to product manufacturers and retailers. Companies like *Procter and Gamble* spend millions every year just understanding the consumer, their needs, their use of products and their shopping behaviour.

The most successful retailers of the last decades, like UK-headquartered *Tesco*, have used loyalty systems to gather data they can analyse to understand consumer needs and target customers more effectively. These are the disciplines that provide a foundation for delivering a differentiated customer experience.

Best practice case: *Tesco*, the UK's most successful grocer and now one of the biggest retail companies globally, transformed itself from number two in the UK market in the early 1990s, into the dramatically growing business it is today, by putting the customer at the centre of its universe. Most important, *Tesco* measured the behaviour of its shoppers by analysing baskets of goods bought, by customer and by store, and converted this information into insights that today guide everything from segment analysis, loyalty management, through range planning, promotions, pricing and store opening plans. *Tesco* creates The Customer Plan based on customer and shopper insights and runs the whole business in line with the plan, with weekly checks and course-corrections. **(More on *Tesco* below)**

But the world is becoming rapidly more complex. Consumer shopping behaviour, like many other aspects of consumer behaviour, is changing rapidly under the influence of the on-line tools they use and experiences they have, in an increasingly global and fast-moving information economy.

Whereas traditionally retailers segmented their customers into typical demographic groups and targeted each of these according to the primary motivators of those groups, there is an increasingly important new layer of motivation on top of these that is driving us towards the "segment of one" or "lifestyle segments". This is not to say these new motivations replace the old, as traditional segmentation is still important, but the new behaviours provide an opportunity for increased customer focus and more targeted responses in addition, leading to happier and more loyal customers.

Let's take an example. Imagine Anna, a typical 18 year old who, like her peers, sees her boyfriend as the most important person in her life, loves spending time on the phone with her closest girlfriends, is very focused on fashion and beauty, loves her music and is deeply concerned about the environment. To this extent she is very similar to many other 18-year-old girls, in line with traditional demographic segmentation models.

In addition, a couple of years ago, Anna signed up to an on-line music management site (examples are *last.fm* and *Pandora;* other on-line music management tools are *Mog, Rhapsody* and Swedish *Spotify*). The intelligent tool on this site interrogated Anna's PC hard drive to identify the styles of music in her music downloads, then searched the internet for all music that matched Anna's music "dna", coming back with a playlist of all the music she might like. Anna was delighted. She could never have got this result without the intelligent on-line tool.

The fact is that Anna, like millions of others, has not only converted to using this sort of value-added tool for her music management, but has done so *in every other area of her life too* – a dramatic lifestyle transformation.

Her college work is all researched and completed on-line, she banks on-line, she participates in environmental groups on-line, communicates and networks via blogs and on-line tools, she browses new fashion trends and catalogues on-line, she shops on *eBay* and increasingly uses value-added aggregator sites that allow her to access catalogues of different retailers according to her preferences (one site matches apparel images, another searches by style). Social networking defines her social circle and activity across countries and groups, providing by far the most powerful influence in her life.

Anna is personalising her world and increasingly is a segment of one, in spite of the overlap of interests and priorities with the rest of her peers in the traditional demographic segment. For example, Anna likes motorbikes, an unusual interest in her age and gender group, and she expresses this in the choice of sites she uses on-line for social networking, managing her leisure time and shopping.

In another traditional segment, Martin, a 35 year old IT manager with a wife and young children, is time poor and also uses on-line tools and intelligent applications to meet his needs for personalising his world and making it more efficient. He books his holiday on-line, participates in a ski forum, files his tax return, manages his investments, and so on. This meets his lifestyle needs.

In both Anna's case and Martin's, access to value-added information and functionality in the on-line world allows them to personalise their worlds to fit their individual needs better, not as a replacement for real world experiences, but as a very pragmatic toolkit. And this is shaping their behaviour both on-line and off-line, including their shopping behaviour.

The reason we see these tools becoming the norm in all ages and demographic groups is that every day, usually via home broadband or personal mobile phone, these consumers are using *Amazon, eBay, Google* and a host of other smart tools for instant and effective management of their worlds. An example of the impact on the bricks and mortar retail world is that consumers are now used to getting instant information on-line (usually within 1-3 seconds) and expect the same response in-store, otherwise they abandon their shop. A common comment from consumers when asked about the in-store world is to say, "It is 2 generations behind what I have on-line at home".

Best practice case (on-line): *Amazon*, pioneering on-line retailer that has expanded from bookseller to general retailer and channel for others, very early on developed and deployed smart real-time tools that track the pattern of use of a consumer when on-line on their site, triggering evolutionary changes in the layout, content and responses of the site to that consumer. Over time, the *Amazon* home-page of an individual *Amazon* user will evolve to more and more

---

closely match their past behaviour and preferences. As a result, no two users of *Amazon* have quite the same home page, especially if they have used the site over a long period. *Amazon* is effectively sensing the needs of the consumer and responding to make the experience more targeted and relevant to that consumer's needs.

Whether your business operates primarily in the traditional bricks and mortar world, on-line, or more likely, in an increasingly *multi*-channel way, the principles remain the same:

- You need a mechanism for **listening** to your customers with a true appreciation for their segment and individual needs,
- You need to use this to **target** those needs more relevantly and effectively, whether with analytics and operational routines or with smart IT tools or both,
- You need to monitor and **measure the impact** of this, so that you can continuously improve your responsiveness.

This is the foundation for delivering a great customer experience: **Understand customer motivation – listen, target, measure.**

Diagram 4:
Understand consumer motivation

Listen – what consumers want today

Consumers today have more options in terms of how they shop than ever before. There is an excess of product information and promotions in multiple channels and wide choices about where and how to shop for almost every category of product or service – in-store, on-line, on-mobile, via catalogue, kiosk or call centre.

In general we all go through five steps in our shopping journey:

- realise need,
- research options,
- compare and select product or service,
- purchase product or service, and,
- seek service.

In the past, these five steps were fairly predictable in terms of where they were completed, because a customer generally had to come to a store to see products, speak to an expert and make the purchase. But in today's multi-channel world, the customer journey can have multiple profiles.

As a retailer, you need to consider:

- How to have visibility of customer activities in different channels (e.g. when researching on-line)?
- How best to support the customer in these multiple places on the journey in ways that are consistent with your brand, yet are non-intrusive?
- How to make it more likely the customer will purchase from you on that journey, rather than from your competitor, irrespective of the specific path they take?

Consider this in the diagram below – here we have three different prompts to a shopping journey, one on television, one on-line and one in the

meeting their lifestyle and needs. It is common to hear a mum say that ten 'o clock at night, when the children are in bed, is the first opportunity in the day to shop. Make it easy, provide many channels.

- **Personalisation:** As we saw from the example of Anna, tools that allow the shopping experience or the activity to be customised to the consumer's specific needs, to be personalised, is valued extremely highly. This is the strongest trend in modern retailing.

- **Security:** With the threat of identity theft ever-present, the consumer expects that you have made provision for a secure transaction. All of the tools are available today to make this possible. (Please note that, to the consumer, this is a necessary hygiene factor, number 5 on their list, whereas many CIOs in retail companies treat it as the number 1 consumer concern.)

So, in today's multichannel shopping world, you will need to measure and monitor these five elements too, alongside the traditional needs, preferably on the same cycle as the channels are used, so that a responsive approach can be taken, clearly signalling to the customer that you are listening.

Best practice case: *Best Buy*, the US-based international consumer electronics retailer, besides demonstrating an acute understanding of the customer's need in consumer electronics to walk away with a working product rather than complex instructions, has put in the mechanisms for responding to the customer's needs. It is the stated objective that customers should leave the store with a working product or the knowledge/support to set it up.

A great example of this is *The Geek Squad* service, where, for a low service fee, the consumer gets access to hands-on expertise in installing, setting up and problem solving their computer and consumer electronics devices. This includes remote diagnostics and repair on the computer, telephone support and on-site visits.

Tools for listening to the consumer:

Tools	Insights
Analyse simple samples of sales data.	General quantitative insights, mainly product based – limited conclusions about the qualitative customer experience.
Conduct focus groups with a sample of target customers; call a sample of customers every week.	Rich qualitative insights that can give early warning of trends, but can be very subjective or skewed and must be repeated frequently.
Talk to your store and contact centre staff to get their insights from direct customer contact.	A rich source of data that provides a qualitative check for the issues the quantitative analysis does not identify.
Conduct desk research on trends via a study of the brands, magazines, TV programmes, films, web sites, celebrities, activities and fashions of the target group.	Very rich qualitative insights that can valuably used throughout the customer experience process, but beware of being too general in your conclusions or putting too much weight on some influences only. Influences and fashions change fast, so keep monitoring.
Use till sales data to apply Business Intelligence for basket analysis.	Strong quantitative and qualitative insights that can guide the business.
Use loyalty data for basket analysis, segmentation and targeting.	The most powerful tool for ongoing listening to the customer – quantitative & qualitative.

Target - focus on the real needs of your consumers

The whole purpose of listening to the customer is so that you can target your offer and your brand experience accordingly. This is the process of turning consumer data into insights and programmes of response.

At the simplest level, if you ran a corner shop, this is something like noticing that at lunch time customers buy a sandwich and a drink, but more people buy sandwiches than drinks in your store. Further investigation might show your drinks assortment to be poor or it might show the drinks cooler placement is poor. Actions could be to review the drinks stocked or to offer a sandwich and drink co-packed promotion at lunch times. The point is that by "listening" to consumer behaviour, you are able to identify an opportunity for providing a better customer offer – result: a more convenient and satisfying customer lunchtime experience, a happier customer and a happier store owner.

In the more complex world of retail chains, the same principle applies, except that now you are working with a lot more data, resulting from your "listening" activities, and grouping customers into segments or clubs of needs is very useful in making it manageable. The disadvantage of traditional segments is that they tend to define people by age, gender and similar criteria, which today do not necessarily define shopping habits. It is therefore better to take actual shopping data and group shoppers into "communities of interest".

Best practice case: *Tesco*, in its *Clubcard* loyalty system, groups its customers into communities of interest or "clubs", according to the mix of groceries they buy. This allows *Tesco* to offer shoppers only those promotions and special offers that are either relevant to their lives or which offer a new experience that logically adds to their current portfolio of interests, consumption and perceived value. This personalised approach demonstrates targeting based on a deep analysis and understanding of customer needs. The result is that, whereas other retailers achieve an average 1% redemption rate on promotional coupons, *Tesco* achieves 30%.

The simple act of analysing needs at a fairly broad level allows *Tesco* very accurately to both meet the needs of its shoppers and to tempt them with new products that have an affinity with those they habitually buy – this is targeting.

Emerging best practice case?: *Borders* USA responded to the threat to its traditional book stores from on-line book-seller *Amazon* and others, by establishing its own on-line presence. When its fortunes continued to dip, it appointed Ron Marshall as CEO to effect a recovery. Under his leadership, the company is has attempted to go one step further than both bricks and mortar and on-line competitors, leveraging its store network, intimate knowledge its customers in local communities and new multi-channel technology tools to create a competitive advantage.

It runs its book clubs, where members receive *Twitter* messages and e-mails according to their chosen genre, attending in-store events and readings and participating in *blogs*, with *podcasts* of author presentations available. Each club is run by a *Borders*' staff member who is passionate about their genre – this may be the CEO or a mailroom clerk. If this succeeds it could well signal the integrated, multi-channel future beyond booksellers.

So, whether you are listening to customers in a very simple way, running a complex analytical programme or keeping close to your customers with an array of modern, interactive tools, the principles remain the same – by listening, you hear people's needs and notice the gaps, targeting is about meeting these needs.

Sometimes the needs will be simple (e.g. "where is my product?") and sometimes they will be much more complex (e.g. "I want to belong to a network of like-minded people"), but *your* challenge is to address those needs in the way best suited to *your* brand proposition and *your* economic model (how you make your money). This warrants some comment.

If you own the corner shop, your brand proposition is very likely about

Let's be clear at this stage. What is described above is the foundation of the differentiated customer experience process, but it is just the foundation. If you are running a traditional loyalty programme where points are awarded to shoppers as rewards for shopping volume or frequency, then this falls into this basic level, facilitating fundamental understanding of the behaviour and needs of your customers and responding to them with rewards targeted at their needs. There is much more needed if you want to create and deliver a great customer experience that will generate true loyalty.

Tools for measuring the impact of targeting the consumer:

Repeat use of the tools for listening to the consumer in the first place. In the case of loyalty programmes, the most powerful listening tool, this should in any case be an ongoing or rolling process.

Tools for articulating your customer targeting strategy

If we look at the brand it is possible to identify the key areas of development in the relationship with the consumer – a roadmap for the development of the brand. This will subtly change the targeting strategy and tactics over time in the same way that a consumer product will gradually evolve over the years. Think of a washing powder brand and its small changes in formula, fragrance, packaging etc. each year. These evolutions are at the heart of your brand and you will manage them over time.

In addition, however, there are bigger trends that pull our targeting strategy in one direction or another. Consider the dramatic growth of on-line shopping and social network sites. In retailing you ignore these at your peril.

There are three areas in which the trends are pulling retail brands at the moment:

- **Differentiated customer experiences:** In a society where consumers have information, smart tools and experiences at their fingertips, whether on-line or on-TV, consumers are increasingly asking for a more memorable shopping experience in order to tempt them into the shopping malls, rather than just cruising the internet. A good example of successful delivery of a unique experience is the use by retailers like *H&M* of celebrities like Madonna to design fashion ranges. The consumer feels they are sharing in the "celebrity experience", especially when the celebrity attends the launch.

- **Self-service:** As consumers have had access to an increasing number of smart tools, this has allowed them to express their preference for managing their own experiences, their own pace of shopping, etc., leading to an explosion of self-service shopping, whether on-line, on-mobile or at self-service points within the store. This holds opportunities for the retailer, but also the dangers that you either lose control of the customer experience or face competition from others who offer better self-service tools. For example, if a supermarket gives me an on-mobile tool for scanning barcodes and managing my grocery shopping list against their product assortment, this set of self-service tools could easily entice me away from my regular supermarket and lock me into using the new one, especially if they also offer home delivery.

- **Consumer generation/self-creation:** Another consequence of smarter tools in the hands of consumers is that they have more opportunity than ever before to express their creativity, a deep-seated need in most people to shape their world.

These trends or opportunity areas are usefully depicted in the following **Customer Experience Analysis & Planning Grid**, a tool for mapping your current and future targeting strategy and tactics, with implications for business organisation, processes and systems that must support them. The zone of multi-channel is to the left of the broken line, but this is migrating to the right as more products and services are offered over the internet, via mobile services and through other channels, as indicated by the arrow. The "social networking" box is a broad area within which people are more likely to engage with others in social activities. To the right hand side this may include physical networking (e.g. meeting up in a coffee shop), whereas to the left it indicates on-line social networks (e.g. *Facebook)*.

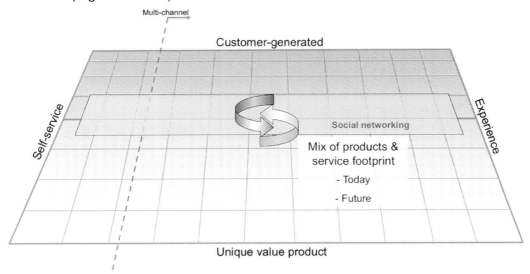

Diagram 8: A grid for analysing and depicting targeting strategy

Using this grid, the emphasis of your targeting strategy will be in one or more of four areas, which are a combination of the four sides of the grid:

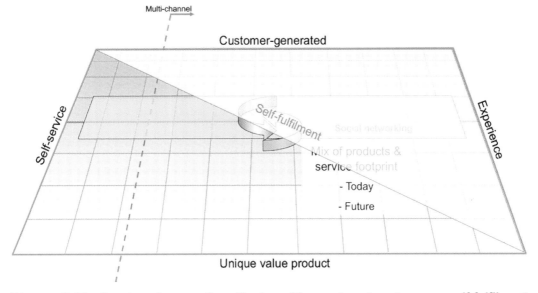

Diagram 9: The four broad areas of positioning with your target customers – self-fulfilment

Combining a great and memorable customer experience and creating an environment in which the consumer can express their creativity or explore their aspirations provides for customers who value self-fulfilment highly. This is usually a face-to-face experience and high-end spas and personal shoppers/fashion advisors traditionally occupy this space.

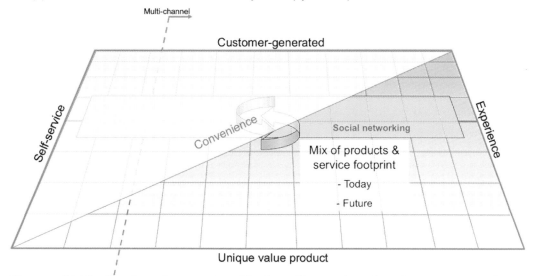

Diagram 10: The four broad areas of positioning with your target customers - convenience

When you combine a strong focus on meeting customers' custom needs and providing them with the self-service tools to meet those needs, you are targeting people who highly value convenience. This quite naturally includes a high amount of multi-channel access to on-line and other automated tools. On-line services like *iTunes* and *last.fm* are great examples of this convenience positioning and grocery home shopping tends in this direction too.

Focusing on those customers who value access to your unique product or service highly can be increasingly satisfied using self-service tools today. This "access" positioning is typical of coffee shops like *Starbucks* on the high street and *Google* on-line.

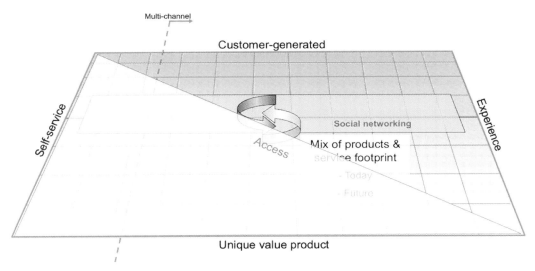

Diagram 11: The four broad areas of positioning with your target customers - access

Finally, customers who focus on the unique value you bring want to engage with the entire brand experience in accessing your product in a service-rich environment, where the shopping experience is the channel to the valued product. High-end fashion labels like *Dior* and *Chanel* occupy this position traditionally.

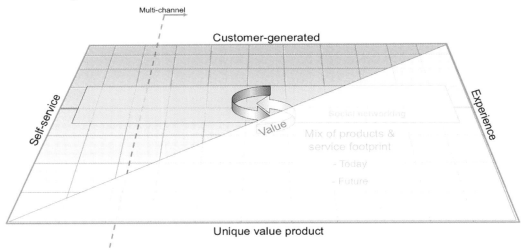

Diagram 12: The four broad areas of positioning with your target customers - value

In this way you will consider how your product and service positioning today can develop in any of the three directions of current trends – experience, self-service, customer generation – and these may change over time.

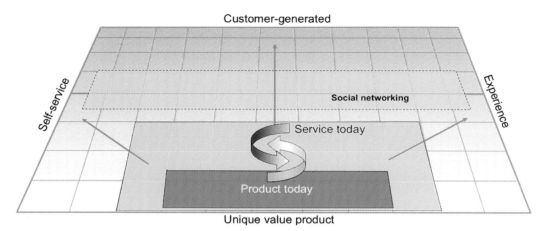

Diagram 13: Three trends we can exploit in our future targeting

Of course this is not as simple as just selecting the areas of emphasis for the future and assuming you can act in this different way towards your customers without some significant adjustments to your organisation, processes and systems, especially as multi-channel becomes an increasing part of the business mix. This implies selecting the future targeting profile, identifying the target mix of organisation, processes and systems and creating a realistic **Customer Service Roadmap** to achieving them.

The following diagram shows just a sample of the sorts of processes, tools and services that could be deployed across the grid, indicating also how the multi-channel portion of the grid increases over time.

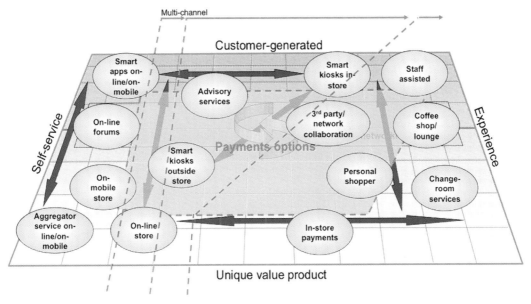

Diagram 14: A sample of future processes, services and tools

Below are a few examples of how I have analysed some well-known brands against this grid (these are purely my views). These show how today's **Brand Grid Footprint**, which is generally concentrated down at the front, bottom end of the grid, can be understood in terms of that particular brand's current targeting and support a discussion of how this might be developed in future.

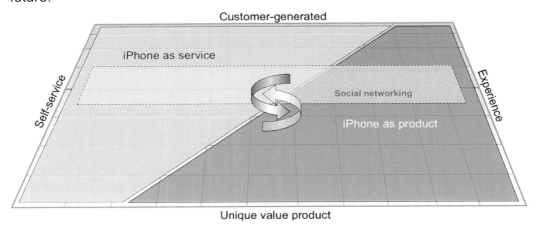

Diagram 15: Why *Apple's iPhone* is so successful?

An American retailer called *Ridemakerz* has established a store that simulates a factory production environment, where fathers and sons or groups of children can produce customised radio-controlled cars, selecting from thousands of optional parts on the production line. I will say more about this innovative retailer in subsequent chapters.

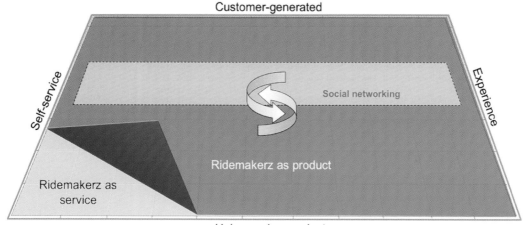

Diagram 16: The *Ridemakerz'* profile?

By contrast, a high-end perfume brand like *Jo Malone*, majors on the experience of a unique product, but has introduced a nice twist in making the fragrances able to be blended by the consumer to create unique new fragrances.

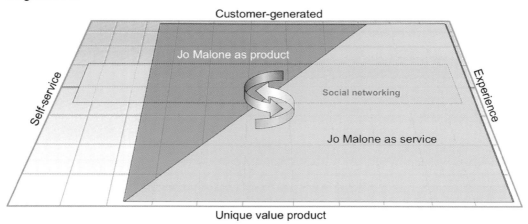

Diagram 17: The *Jo Malone* profile?

The London department store *Selfridge & Co,* recently crowned best department store in the world (2010), is a model of delivering a value-added and unique environment within which the world's brands can showcase their value for customers. *Selfridges* is about the experience.

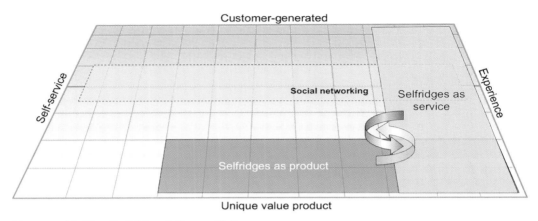

Diagram 18: The *Selfridge & Co* profile?

In fashion, *The Gap*, like most of its successful competitors, holds a favoured position in the eyes of its customers because of the unique value products it makes available in the right combination and at the right price point.

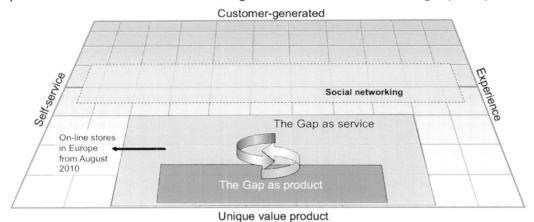

Diagram 19: *The Gap* profile?

An innovator and experimenter in the fashion retailing segment is *Threadless*, a Chicago-based on-line and store chain that gets its t-shirts designed by its customers, in return for payment if the design is accepted and a bigger payment if it sells well.

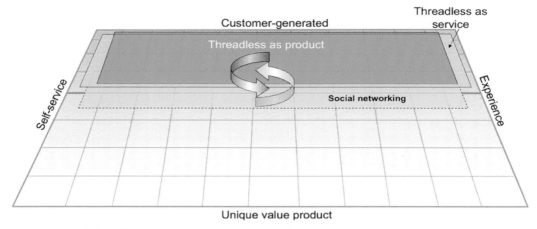

Diagram 20: *Threadless* **is leveraging customers' need to be creative**

A useful exercise for you would be to map your current **Product and Service Positioning** on the grid and use this as a starting point for discussing into which areas of the grid you should extend over time, both to keep existing customers and to target new ones.

Once you are effectively targeting your customers, you need to measure the effect.

Traditional loyalty programmes and their role in shaping the customer experience:

Given the powerful role that loyalty programmes, customer databases and analytics can have in understanding and targeting customers effectively, it is worth spending some time outlining their history and role in this process.

Loyalty programmes have gone through several generations since their inception 80 years ago, with most development having taken place in the last 20-25 years, in tandem with modern technology.

From the outset they were perceived as ways of rewarding customers for shopping in your stores in proportion to the frequency and/or size of spend – a mechanism for retaining and growing existing customers through incentives. Over time this has become more complex and sophisticated and loyalty programmes today are used for business planning, store assortment decisions, category management and much more, in addition to customer loyalty management itself.

Because understanding the customer depends on listening, analysing and targeting, as well as measuring the impact on customer behaviour, it is worth considering the role traditional and modern loyalty programmes have to play in this.

1st generation loyalty – coupons, instant rewards and promotions:

In the earliest loyalty programmes simple reward mechanisms were introduced – coupons or loyalty points – to ensure there was an instant response to the shopper behaviour we wanted to reinforce.

As early as 1929 in the USA, *General Mills' Betty Crocker* brand of flour inserted coupons in packages. These could be used to redeem cooking ingredients and cookware. By the 1930s the coupons were printed on the outside of packages. Later still, the programme produced a reward catalogue from which customers could pick rewards using their points. This highly successful and popular early loyalty programme ended in 2006, after 77 years, having provided the blueprint for most modern loyalty programmes. The *S&H Green Stamps* were also a popular retail reward coupon from the 1930s through the 1980s. Typically, as a customer shopped at various stores, she would receive a set number of *Green Stamps* that could be pasted into booklets and redeemed for prizes.

Later loyalty schemes built on these early programmes. For example, the airline industry realised in the early 1980s that they were flying many routes with some empty seats. These seats could be offered as rewards to loyal customers and, without increasing costs at all, the seat could be filled with a delighted "frequent flyer" and simultaneously recognised as a marketing promotional cost, rather than simply an operating cost.

In 1981, *American Airlines* launched the first modern loyalty programme with its *AAdvantage* frequent flyer programme, a programme that now has over 50 million members. As with other airline programmes, rewards are given in reward "air miles".

From the 1980s to the present day, loyalty programmes have had a profound effect on the modern shopper. Most consumers today carry a loyalty card from their preferred airline, hotel chain or supermarket, and frequently carry multiple cards. Credit cards have become linked to loyalty schemes to the extent that half of all US credit card users use a points-based rewards programme.

In retail, these 1st generation loyalty programmes, where instant reward through points and promotions are the primary function, are today still common in all parts of the world, but probably most consistently and actively applied in the French grocery retailers like *Carrefour, Auchan* and *Casino*, as well as in the specialty and department stores in Italy, though we have begun to see some shift more recently towards mixing these with an emphasis on analytics insights.

From a technology point of view, simple coupon and points-based systems need very little. In the *Betty Crocker* world physical coupons were redeemed for rewards. Frequent flyer records log "air miles" and match these to flights or other rewards redeemed in the simplest systems. In the French hypermarkets the instant points awarded at the till are redeemed for a discount, while accumulated points are redeemed via a central database.

Understandably, it did not take long for retailers and others to recognise that the customer shopping data associated with the loyalty programme is a potential gold mine of customer and shopper insights – a tool for listening more accurately to the customer, so that targeting can be more accurate, where responses to promotional activity can be quickly and accurately measured. But this needed more complex tools for data management and analysis.

2nd generation loyalty – analysis and the problem of data:

Through the 1980s and into the 1990s we saw a proliferation of loyalty schemes and the first attempts to systematically analyse shopping data to gain insights for targeting customers with loyalty or promotional offers.

While early insights were powerful, as data proliferated there was a realisation that a technical and practical challenge existed in being able to store, manage, analyse and sensibly use the mass of customer data streaming in every day.

So, while many companies struggled during this period to cope with the data monster they had created, what we also saw was the development of the first smarter loyalty and relationship management applications and, most importantly, the deployment of business intelligence tools to begin mining the data collected. This was to prove the catalyst for the golden age of traditional loyalty programmes from 1995 onwards.

3rd generation loyalty and the "club" concept:

> **Best practice – Loyalty:** No company better demonstrates the power, process and tools of effective customer loyalty programmes than *Tesco*, which was the UK's number 2 retailer until 1994, when it overtook the UK market leader through a carefully executed new strategy, growing its business locally and then globally over the next 15 years to become the world's 4th largest retailer.

Tesco began investigating the benefit of a loyalty card in 1993, by collecting data from customers and then sending them targeted offers. In 1994, the man responsible for *Tesco's* trials, Grant Harrison, attended a conference where Clive Humby from *dunnhumby* was speaking. *dunnhumby* had been founded in 1989, using data analytics to target marketing services for companies like *BMW*.

The first response from *Tesco's* then-Chairman Lord MacLaurin to the initial *dunnhumby* analysis was, "What scares me about this is that you know more about my customers after three months than I know after 30 years." *Clubcard* was launched in 1995 and has 7 million members in the UK today, in addition to mirror schemes in other countries in which Tesco operates.

The essence of the *Clubcard* concept is implied in the name – shopping and product purchase patterns are classified into "clubs" that indicate "communities of interest". In this way someone buying wines frequently is placed in the "wine club", the buyer of baby goods can be in the "baby club" and the buyer of dog food is in the "pet club". Simultaneous membership of various "clubs" creates broad segments of club clusters. In this way, promotions can be targeted accurately at club members to provide incentives to continue shopping that category at *Tesco*, promotions to extend their penetration in the category or to try out related club offers.

Increasingly sophisticated analysis of the patterns of shopping within each club (e.g. buying economy packs versus premium products) can also be used to shape the promotions to the customer more accurately. It is these analytics and club-based responses that make it possible for Tesco to achieve a 30% redemption rate on mailed coupons, while traditional, untargeted coupons are lucky to get a 1% redemption rate.

More sophisticated analytics systems, a simple club-based concept and increasing use of specialised campaign management software took loyalty programmes into a new and powerful era, where it is possible to "listen" very accurately to customer shopping behaviour, target customers very accurately with relevant offers and measure in near real-time how well the targeting is working.

Increasing sophistication in the application of Business Intelligence has taken this yet one step further more recently.

4th generation loyalty and the "dna" concept:

Having analysed shopping data from a shopper point of view and created a shopper "dna" of clubs, products, price points, times of month, week and day and so forth, it was not a big leap to turn this around and analyse the same data in other dimensions - by category, by store, by season, etc.

Categories of product can be analysed across the shopper base to understand the impact of different quality, price point, branding and availability on different types of shopper. Category analytics has become an important part of the output of loyalty programmes, guiding sourcing and procurement managers within the category teams, as well as their colleagues that must optimise pricing, for example.

In this way, a retailer is able to offer an assortment of products in a particular store that is shaped to the historical patterns of the shoppers who use the store, plus promotions and innovations that might match their needs. When combined with demographic data about the area in which the store is located, this becomes even more powerful for attracting new shoppers to your stores. Stores begin to have an assortment "dna", based on loyalty data analysis and insights.

Next generation loyalty – customer managed tools:

It is important to note that the tools and practices of each generation of loyalty have added something to the toolkit. Each of these approaches and their tools are still valuable today, whether used alone or in combination. Indeed sometimes the simpler 1st generation loyalty programmes are more suited to specific market conditions, and sometimes different generations of tools can operate effectively simultaneously.

Choosing your loyalty portfolio is specific to your business profile.

Next generation loyalty deploys modern tools of Web 2.0, social networking and increasingly the mobile phone as both portal and customer recognition device – this will be discussed at the end of the section after the next: *Deliver attainable lifestyle dreams.*

The 2nd pillar: Engage the consumer community

So you are listening to customers to understand their needs, targeting your customers with your value proposition aligned to those needs and measuring the results, not least through the sales you achieve. This is necessary in order to have a sustainable retail business and it is the foundation of the whole differentiated customer experience process, but it is just the beginning.

We now need to build on that foundation of understanding and response by engaging the consumer community at a deeper, emotional level. Some of this is about information, but much more is about empowerment and engagement at that emotional level, that will simultaneously bind you to the community you serve and dramatically deepen your understanding of their needs – the needs that, when satisfied, prompt true brand loyalty.

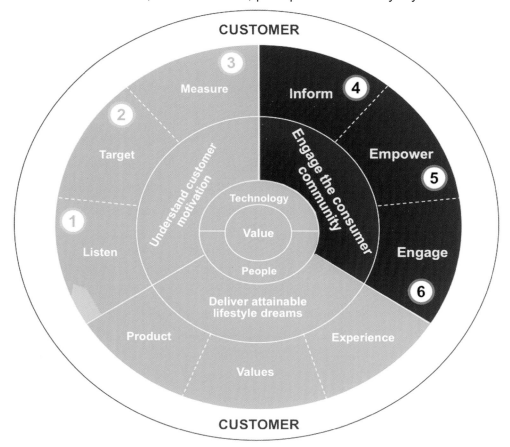

Diagram 21: Engage the consumer community

Best practice case (traditional store): Mexican department store *El Palacio de Hierro* focuses, amongst other things, on up-market fashion. Listening to its women customers, it realised that there is a sub-culture of "being a woman", built on extensive shared experience of the world, social attitudes and the way women are regarded by men and society at large. Based on these insights, *El Palacio de Hierro* began communicating with its target audience, "the tribe of women" with an advertising campaign that was designed to inform the customer of the products, values and ambience of the company, but more importantly, to share an empowering message that engaged the women in a shared community around *El Palacio de Hierro* fashion.

Typical advert messages were, for example, "There are two questions a man never knows how to answer – do you love me? and, do I look good in this?". There is also clever use of visual imagery that taps into the sub-conscious of "being a woman", such as a woman diving into a pool, where designer shoes drift towards the bottom, or another where a naked woman is seen to love her shoes so much she has taken a bite out of one.

See several good examples of these adverts on *YouTube*.

It so happens that the best practice example above used print and television advertising extensively in informing, empowering and engaging the target customers, reinforced by store and on-line experiences consistent with the message and values communicated. Advertising is of course a powerful traditional way of prompting engagement with the customer, but it is just one way and an increasingly ineffective way compared to social media tools in today's increasingly multi-channel world.

In fact, a blend of advertising (various media), social networking, structured experiences and events inside and outside the store, need to be designed to respond to your customers' needs in ways that reflect and communicate the brand values, products and services that resonate with those needs.

Best practice case (new media): Finnish *Seppälä*, a fashion chain owned by the *Stockmann Group* and focused on teens and early twenty year old women, identified through customer surveys that the most cherished dream of their customers is to appear on television. The company launched a "be a model" campaign on their website, where customers can put themselves forward to appear in a *Seppälä* ad.

The candidates are assessed by their peers on-line, with the winners appearing in the ads – social networking used to inform, motivate and engage customers, leading to viral awareness of the brand and its values and a community for whom *Seppälä* is the facilitator for realising their dreams. The campaign has been so successful that youngsters from well beyond the boundaries of Finland are signing up to "be a model" for *Seppälä.*

Go to *seppala.fi* to explore the campaign.

Let's now look in more detail at the three components of engaging the consumer community – *inform, empower, engage.*

Inform the customer

Informing is about signalling to your target customer clearly and in compelling fashion that you share their values and can meet their needs. This extends from the most basic branding decisions like choice of colour, through designs, images and slogans, to the messaging in product displays and other media.

It is at once a feeling and a set of lifestyle and value statements and an overt articulation of the brand promise you offer to your customers.

Best practice case: *The Body Shop* is a great example of how a total value system and lifestyle choice can be simply and effectively projected. As I write, the web-site home page shows a grassy slope, plenty of green and natural images, a casual font that looks like a friend's handwriting and great products well-described and promoted. This has pervaded *The Body Shop* approach from the moment it was set up by Anita Roddick. She caught the trend towards the natural and the organic and was herself passionate about the values and lifestyle *The Body Shop* represented, but this could have been an interesting short-term phenomenon had it not been so well executed. The simple and effective projection of the values of *The Body Shop* in the products, merchandising, advertising, actions and overt messages to the consumer is what makes this a best practice case.

Of course your informing of your customers of who you are, what you represent and what you can offer them starts with your **brand promise** and reflects the insights you have gained from your ongoing *listening, targeting and measurement* activities in *understanding consumer motivation*, as described in the previous section. (These processes have been described sequentially in this text for convenience, but all of the processes are ongoing and intertwined, constantly building on each other).

The question you need to ask is, "How will I communicate to my target customers the brand promise – the values and lifestyle we represent – as embodied in the products and/or services you offer?"

Also, how will I do this in a way that is a response to their needs?

And how will I do it in a way that is compelling, captures their attention and prompts them to actively respond?

Best practice case (contemporary): Spanish fashion retailer *Desigual*, when they launched a new store in Spain, invited their customers to come and paint the store walls with the images, colours and slogans that they wanted – getting the customer to create the message. This clearly communicated the *Desigual* values – personalisation, creativity, involvement, you create the look. This involving approach employed by *Desigual* was the ultimate way of informing its customers of its values and the lifestyle it represents.

See on the *Desigual* website how this graffiti theme is perpetuated today.

Tools for informing the customer:

The process of designing your "inform" step is:

- *Articulate the Brand value proposition:* What do you uniquely represent in your brand, irrespective of the products you sell? For example, a fashion brand focused on teens might define its brand proposition as, "Enabling teenage girls to participate in the celebrity lifestyle".

- *Review the needs of your target customers:* What are the specific needs you have identified by listening to your customers? In the fashion brand mentioned above, these might include, "I want to be recognised", "I want to appear on TV", "I want to be a singer", a whole cluster of **aspiration and recognition** needs common to teenagers today, reflected in the "reality TV" trend that has swept the world in the last ten years, under the influence of the internet.

- *Identify the brand/customer intersection:* What are the core values and lifestyle elements that intersect the brand with the target consumers? This might be all of the attributes of "celebrity fashion", "red carpet events", "reality TV", "*YouTube*", social networking, the txt culture and the celebrity gossip magazines, in our example above,

- *Select media and channels:* Now match the target customer needs, values and lifestyle to media and channels. In our teen fashion example this might include, in addition to regular advertising and billboards, *Facebook*, blogs, on-line fashion applications, celebrity gossip magazines, mobile phone applications and the right TV programmes and events. Celebrities themselves might be the channel. This can be seen in *H&M*, the Swedish fashion retailer that has taken the world by storm, using well-known designers and celebrities to design its off-the shelf range, with massive success. The simple example from *Seppälä*, given in the earlier section, applies here too.

- *Design the "message":* Match the target customer needs, values and lifestyle to the messaging. The message must simply and directly express the values and lifestyle choice the brand represents, preferably visually or iconically, rather than just in words. For example, the *Nike* slogan "just do it" is powerful, but the simple tick logo is just as powerful on its own. It shouts "active, powerful, healthy winner".

Best practice examples mentioned above: *H&M*, *Seppälä*, *Nike*

Empower the customer

Empowering the consumer means giving them access to information, functionality or a place where they can shape their experiences and realise their dreams. If the message is "we share the same values and lifestyle", then empowerment is enabling or providing the opportunity for the consumer to engage in and shape that shared arena.

It is at this point that we begin to shift from marketing to customers towards sharing with them and beginning to deliver the customer experience through making their dreams attainable.

Best practice cases: Let's consider *Ridemakerz*, a US-based workshop store for kids and adults with a passion for model cars, where customers can build customised designs on a mini production line. Dads are effectively given the opportunity and the tools to express "being a Dad" in a way that is easier, effective and satisfying for both father and child. The value "making something together is fulfilling and fun" is turned into reality by the opportunity to build a model car together. More recently the company has extended this to taking the experience to a child's birthday party and recreating the excitement and fun there. **Visit ridemakerz.com to experience the brand message.**

At *The Body Shop* you as customer are given access to all sorts of information on communities around the world, natural cosmetics and cosmetic ingredients, the opportunity to support good causes and the tools for creating, storing and using your own natural and sustainable cosmetics portfolio. These are the tools that turn the values and lifestyle choices the brand represents into something attainable. The customer can engage in the brand.

A good recent example of empowerment of the consumer through the engagement process comes from *Borders USA*. When Bill Clinton launched a new book, it was announced to members of *Borders'* Politics Book Club members via a personal e-mail to all of them from Bill Clinton. Not only are they reading about politics, they are engaging with political leaders, courtesy of *Borders*. They are beginning to realise their attainable dream.

Once you have informed your target customers through the right media and messaging of your brand value proposition and empowered them through access to the right tools and opportunities, you need to engage with them in an active, ongoing process that evolves the brand and binds the customers to it.

Tools for empowering the customer

The customer is empowered by access to value-added information and functionality. Examples of channels for these you can provide to your customers are:

Value-added information:

- *Print and on-line:* Suitable for the basic brand message and utility information ("How do I?", "Instructions", etc.).

- *News flashes, SMS and Twitter messages:* Suitable for alerts, short updates or "gossip".

- *Newsletters, social media such as* Facebook *and blogs:* Suitable for deeper updates and brand-building, where a dialogue can be established, networks created and events organised.

Value-added functionality:

- *On-line applications:* These are usually applications that help the customer to select the right product or service for their need or design a solution. Good examples are the interior design tools for designing a new kitchen or bathroom or the decorating and costing toolkit found on *mydeco.com*. Aggregators have often led the way in developing these – investment comparison sites, holiday/vacation sites, used goods resale sites (e.g. *eBay*) and increasingly the fashion aggregation sites. The tool on *anthropologie.com* for sorting the clothing and accessories catalogue by colour is a great example of a value-added tool that really meets the consumers' needs better.

- *On-mobile applications:* The mobile phone is becoming the channel of choice for value-added functionality, mainly because it is mobile and the functionality is accessible at the point of need. In addition to accessing on-line applications from the smart phone, there are all of the smart phone applications available too, from grocery shopping tools like the one from *Ocado* in the UK to consumer electronics search engines and a myriad others. What will truly and simply add value to your customer's shopping journey?

- *On-kiosk applications:* All of the on-line services can be delivered on-kiosk and kiosks can also be programmed to provide value-added support at the shelf – think of *L'Oreal's* beauty advisor kiosk integrated with the make-up display. What support at-shelf will add most value to your customer?

- *Staff:* Don't forget that staff will be the first and last point of contact in many cases, whether directly in a store, via on-line or a call centre. They need to be comprehensively trained in all brand and value-added information and equipped with the same tools the consumer can access. There is nothing worse for a sales assistant than standing in the store unsupported by ready information, while facing a customer who is accessing on-line information from the company site and comparison sites. Equip your people!

Engage the customer

Engaging is about drawing the customer into an interactive, ongoing relationship, driven by the customer's recognition of common values and lifestyle attributes in the retail brand.

Do not be fooled, relationship here lasts as long as the resonance between the customer and the brand continue – **Brand Resonance**. A brand that goes off-message or transforms itself into something different will shed loyal consumers. Similarly, people pass through different phases and life stages, so will naturally move on from youth-oriented brands to others, for example.

The key to initiating engagement is achieving the largest degree of resonance between the values and lifestyle attributes of your target customers and the brand. Once the engagement is initiated, then you must sustain this with messages, a media mix, interaction opportunities, stores' experiences, etc. that continuously reinforce the *brand resonance*.

Best practice case: Let us consider *El Palacio de Hierro* again, the up-market Mexican department store group mentioned earlier. In defining themselves in terms of "the tribe of women", they created a resonance with women around Mexico, all of whom immediately recognised that this retailer had taken the time to understand the deepest and most hidden feelings and experiences of women in modern Mexico.

Because they identify with the empowering values and empathetic description of women's needs, the customers engage enthusiastically with the brand. The stores are not selling anything other than shoes, lingerie, fashion clothing, cosmetics, etc., if we look at products, but what they are really selling is the sense of community engendered in women by their brand, as well as the ways to satisfy those real needs through the products on sale.

As this is a critical moment in the entire process of delivering the customer experience, the moment of engagement, it is worth pausing and considering a few more best practice examples, so that it is very clear what is required at this moment in the process.

There are a number of established brands that have built their reputations and indeed their places in the modern culture on the basis of a deep understanding of how to delight customers, creating a truly great customer experience.

Best practice case study: A great case that everyone will recognise is *Disney*, the company that took Walt Disney's delight with a simple cartoon mouse and translated it into a magical world of entertainment and wonder for children and adults globally. Look closely and you will see all of the ingredients of the customer experience process described here.

Disney understands the child in all of us, targets that sense of fun and fantasy and actively measures the impact on people numerous qualitative ways, in addition to tracking things like entertainment park visits and film theatre tickets sold.

The *Disney* message is a clear invitation to be entertained, to engage with larger than life characters in the cartoons or light-hearted stories that demonstrate the importance of good community values – a wholesome image that delivers wholesome fun and a great experience. This engages people of all ages around the world in a quite unique way.

It is however not just the large and well-established brands that are getting it right. There are a number of small start-ups and newer chains that are doing a great job at projecting a brand that engages target customers effectively.

> **Best practice case:** *Ridemakerz,* the model car store chain that we touched on earlier in this section, is a good example of effective customer engagement, in spite of just 12 stores and a regional footprint. When you go on the web-site you can immediately feel the passion for model cars. The stores are little workshops every boy (small or large!) dreams of having. Parents and children alike are drawn to the creative and satisfying experience of making a car.

A final couple of examples of engaging the consumer effectively can be found in the heart of London's Oxford Street – *Selfridge & Co* – and on the web, out of Chicago – *Threadless.com*.

> **Best practice example:** *Selfridge & Co* has been operating in the UK since 1909 and has always promised a unique and exciting shopping experience, constantly surprising its customers with daring events and promotions that sometimes shock, sometimes titillate and always delight.
>
> The window displays of the landmark London store are used to good effect to communicate directly with shoppers the themes and promotions of the moment, drawing people from far and wide. Students of design, other retailers and customers all enthusiastically look forward to the new window displays at *Selfridges*. The windows are the visible "inform" signal that creates the anticipation in customers that they can come in for a great experience, empowered to enjoy themselves, engaged with the brand.
>
> The brand says "touch me, feel me, experience the pampering luxury – let go a little, fantasise and enjoy yourself" and thousands of shoppers every week respond and do just that.

On the high street you have the benefit of being able to physically dress windows and attract the attention of passing trade, building a reputation and becoming a destination. Location is very important.

By contrast, web businesses have to work very hard to create a compelling reason for shoppers to visit and then return again and again in the faceless space of the internet. A like-minded community, a personalised experience and empowering activities and functionality are all essential in creating successful customer engagement.

Best practice example (multi-channel): The *Threadless.com* business is a great example of "collaborative innovation", where an on-line community creates T-shirt designs, selects the ones to sell by democratic vote and rewards the designers.

This retailer, which also has stores, leverages the needs of the modern shopper for social networking and peer recognition, provides a channel for creativity and rewards participants too. This is a great example of successful customer engagement.

Go to *Threadless.com* to experience the brand

In this section I have focused more on examples, as this better illustrates successful customer engagement than conceptual descriptions.

The real challenge thereafter is to deliver on the brand promise – no amount of listening, targeting, measuring, informing, empowering and engaging with the customer will create a sustainable brand unless the actual customer experience consistently delivers on the promise. This is the subject of Section 3: *Deliver attainable lifestyle dreams*.

Tools for engaging the customer:

Tool	Impact
Advertising	Ideally the advert should invite the customer in a compelling way to engage, using the imagery of the sub-culture or attributes of the lifestyle the brand represents. Link this to an event or opportunity to participate.
Displays	Displays draw customers to a destination to engage with the brand. Displays like the window displays of *Selfridges* in London, are reasons to visit, a fun opportunity to be surprised and delighted by the design itself, as well as by the scale, the ambition and the creativity of the displays. Having a celebrity appear in your store can also be regarded as a "display" – creating a spectacle that draws the consumer in.
Events	In today's stay-at-home culture, where vast amounts of time are spent on-line, an event is one of the things that will draw people to the malls, especially teenagers. Like displays, this is often about making celebrity accessible or creating a spectacle on a scale that delights people. It is especially good if participants are able to interact with each other, creating a shared experience within a like-

	minded community.
	Of course events can take place on-line too, using social networking sites, messenger and blog technology. The benefit of on-line events is that they can cut across geographic borders and are easily accessible to all.
Opportunities to participate	Like events, opportunities to participate invite customers to share experience with like-minded people, but add the dimension of peer recognition (see *Threadless.com* example above), personalisation and a sense of shaping the experience. This is truly active engagement.

The 3rd pillar: Deliver attainable lifestyle dreams

In the "engaging the customer" stage of the process described in the previous section, we already began to deliver the customer experience. The customer experience is a journey that starts at awareness and continues right through the retail experience and beyond.

Here we will focus primarily on that part of the customer experience which is the store or purchase experience itself. Let's illustrate with an example.

Best practice case: *Apple* is a great brand, with clear positioning and great products, translated into a great retail experience. So what makes this succeed?

Apple people are enthusiasts of the simple and effective ways *Apple* technology works and this means that every product exemplifies the values and lifestyle attributes of the typical *Apple* customer. When translated into a retail environment, this means:

- A clean, uncluttered work space
- Futuristic, simple design values
- Information at your fingertips
- Support from staff or a handy video guide just a request away, whether in-store or on-line; training on demand,
- Products available at home, from the store or as a download
- Personalisation of your portfolio, from *iPod* colour to desktop design
- No queues, no fuss, easy payment and an e-mail receipt

The *Apple* retail experience combines a pleasant and user-friendly *experience*, the *Apple values* and great *products* – that is why it was voted by retailers world-wide in 2009 the *Global Retailer of the Year*.

And that really is what the great customer experience is about – the experience itself must be unique or satisfying, but it is also the values expressed in that experience and the product or service quality itself that makes it truly great. Achieving the synchronisation of experience, values and product is the essence of the final stage of our process – *delivering the attainable lifestyle dream*.

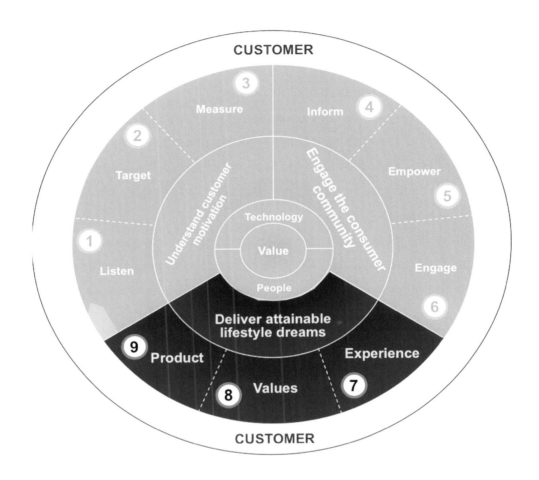

Diagram 22: Deliver attainable lifestyle dreams

In this section I will try to separate the delivery of attainable lifestyle dreams into the three components of *experience*, *values* and *product*, but I must emphasise that these are three dimensions of a continuum that together comprise the differentiated and sustainable customer experience. Creating a memorable experience without clear values is a temporary experience at best, while creating an experience without the support of a quality product or service range is simply unsustainable. Even more than this, *the product is an extension of the experience.*

Experience

A great experience is one that is emotionally engaging because it opens up new possibilities, uniquely expresses your person interests, values or personality or offers something so new, unexpected and pleasurable that it surprises and delights you. It puts something aspirational within reach – this is what we mean by creating attainable dreams.

The best way of demonstrating this is via some good examples, so below you will find a series of examples from different segments of retailing, followed by some further analysis and an overview of tools you can use to shape great experiences – and don't forget the great consumer electronics example of *Apple* above.

Most of the examples used under the heading "experience", could also be used under the headings "values" and "product", so do explore the examples given in their broadest context, in addition to the points they illustrate here.

Best practice cases:

Department store: In the case of *Selfridge & Co*, used earlier to illustrate customer engagement through the promise of a great customer experience and the use of innovative window displays, the brand lives up to that promise, offering a rich experience across multiple luxury brands and categories, with coffee shop and restaurant opportunities and high end food products on multiple floors of its flagship store. Consumers walk away from a *Selfridges* shopping experience carrying the very visible yellow *Selfridges* shopping bag as a satisfying badge of achievement.

Fashion: The Swedish fashion chain *H&M* frequently teams up with well-known designers to create affordable ranges of young women's clothing. The stores are mobbed when these are released and ranges sell out quickly. This is an example of creating the chance to "share in celebrity".

On-line this is taken to an extreme of speed and responsiveness in on-line fashion retailer *ASOS* ("as seen on screen"). *ASOS*, as a pure on-line fashion store, has grown in 9 years to close to £100m p.a. in turnover.

Entertainment: _Disney_ too consistently lives up to its brand promise, delivering great entertainment for all the family, built on reliable values – exactly what was promised in the "engagement" process.

Multi-channel: In the multi-channel arena there are many great shopping experiences in addition to _ASOS_ mentioned above, including _Ridemakerz,_ the model car production line that can be used on-line or in-store and _Threadless,_ the collaborative t-shirt design company that uses and rewards consumers for creating winning t-shirt designs.

One of the most interesting multi-channel services trialled are the _Nike_ on-line and the _Reebok_ on-mobile trainer design and order services, a great way of engaging the trendy youngster who wants to design his own gear. A great creative experience leads to a personalised product that stays with you for months, constantly reminding you of the great experience the brand made possible.

So what makes these experiences great? _It is that they are all relevant, engaging, needs-focused and consistent, they are repeatable and they are supported by a clear set of brand values._

To illustrate, let me give an example of an experience that is not relevant and so fails to delight the consumer. A well-known brand of spirits decided to open a retail outlet that would offer a unique customer experience, showcase the history of the brand and uses of the product.

A sophisticated experience was designed, where shoppers could interactively explore the history of the brand, blend their own drinks in-store with automated support and even create personalised labels for their own gift bottle of the drink. Although all of the elements of a good modern retail experience are present – the opportunity to actively engage, an avenue for creativity, personalisation, etc. – the experience offered is simply not that relevant to most modern consumers and, more importantly, _the experience is not relevant to the brand, which traditionally centres on the concept of "participating in an age-old tradition"._

As a tourist gimmick this may work, but as a sustainable brand experience, it does not. So beware of taking a mechanical approach to constructing a retail customer experience, as brand relevance, values consistency and product integrity must be retained intact at the heart of the experience

Tools for shaping the customer experience

1. The customer experience checklist:

- *Relevance:* Always ask if the experience you are designing for your customer is relevant to their needs (customer relevance) and to the core values of your brand (brand relevance). Being too generic or superficial, as in the drinks company example above, will alienate your best customers.
  - o The best way of testing *customer relevance* is asking the question, "If my most loyal target customer named an aspirational experience, would this be it?" How closely you approximate to the actual aspirational experiences of your core customers is a measure of relevance. In the case of the Finnish fashion retailer *Seppälä*, creating the opportunity for their teenage customers to appear on TV in *Seppälä* ads created an opportunity to make an aspirational experience an actual one.
  - o The best way of testing brand relevance is by comparing the descriptors of your brand essence with a description of the experience. If you imagine the brand as a person, with its essence, values and lifestyle attributes, would it engage in this as a preferred activity or experience? For example, *Disney* as a brand would potentially fit well with a "Mad Hatter's Tea Party" event, aimed at children and their parents, but not with a teenage rave party, featuring a trendy line-up of live bands.
- *Engagement:* What is the level of engagement required of the customer to

---

take part in the experience?

- o *Passive customers* simply experiencing an environment can help to create a mood or set the context for the brand, but at some point there must be a prompt to more active engagement to truly offer a memorable customer experience.

- o *Somewhat active experiences* are sometimes counter-productive, as you are asking for a response from the customer, but not expecting much. This low energy approach can be more damaging than a clear passive experience.

- o The best engagement occurs when *customers must actively shape the experience*, in response to the environment and tools provided by the retailer. In the case of *Desigual*, the Spanish fashion label, this takes the form of stores in Barcelona merchandised as if they are market stalls, with clothing items hung like hams from the ceiling and accessories in wooden trays like vegetables. It is an invitation to touch, feel, engage with and explore the "produce", to engage with the fashion, something *Desigual's* customers enthusiastically do.

- *Needs-focus:* Ask the question, "Can the experience be directly mapped to the aspirational needs of the core target customers?" For example, when *last.fm* (or other similar sites) invites on-line users to download its business intelligent music manager, it creates a "wow" experience when it delivers the playlist that so closely matches the customer's music tastes.

- *Consistent and repeatable, supported by a clear set of brand values:* Always test the planned experience against the brand values, the quality of the experience last time and therefore the consistency of what the customer is experiencing when they come back again and again.

- *And finally:* How will the experience surprise and delight the consumer?

2. Some notes on next generation loyalty programmes and tools – value added information and applications on-line and on-mobile:

As consumers have become empowered through access to smart tools on the internet – *Google, eBay, Facebook, last.fm, YouTube* etc. – they have become impatient with processes that dictate to them or simply push promotions at them. The result is that loyalty programmes are shifting away from being primarily points and promotions-based rewards systems, towards being programmes that offer access to *value-added information and functionality*.

In this way, the reward for being a member of a grocery retailer's loyalty programme is, instead of points or discounts only, though these may still be there, access to the tools that make life easier. For example, having access to an on-line or on-mobile tool for managing my shopping list, may be more valuable to me in saved time than a discount on my next washing powder purchase. Innovative high- end grocers like *Waitrose* in the UK have launched sophisticated applications for their customers.

Traditional loyalty programmes are of course also venturing into the interactive world where mobile phones become the device of choice, even at the simplest level of recognition; e.g. *Tesco* has recently launched a simple *iPhone* application so that points can be collected by shoppers by presenting a barcode on the handset, instead of a keyfob or card. *Tesco* has also recently launched a "click-and-collect" service in partnership with *Nokia*.

See more at techfortesco.blogspot.com

Values

A brand's values are like a good friend to the consumer – familiar, aspirational ideals that represent aspects of the life and lifestyle the consumer would ideally like to have.

At one end of the scale this may be about the simple utility of a milkman delivering milk to the front door, or it may be more complex, as in the purchase of organic vegetables delivered straight from the farm, or even at the most complex end of the scale, a woman choosing the fashion items that will define her look, the inward and outward expression of her personality. These are just the visible "purchase level" components of the brand experience; the real values are buried in the layers beneath.

Let's take the purchase of organic vegetables delivered straight from the farm. The values expressed in this choice are a combination of some or all of the following, amongst others:

- A connection to the earth
- Back to basics
- Health and vitality
- Purity
- Caring for the earth, conserving
- Sustaining the rural community
- Self-sufficiency in the community
- Choice
- Convenience

These can be expressed in the product and supporting services, but they also suggest the repertoire of customer experiences that would be relevant for the consumer. They suggest the colours, logos, messages, activities, causes and experiences that should or could be the expression of the brand.

As Tom Ford emphasised in talking about a store experience – everything must synchronise: what you see, smell, hear; the colours, combinations and more, into a total experience that unambiguously expresses the values that comprise the brand. This is as true on-line as in the store, even though the levers are more limited.

Best practice case: Perfume brand *Jo Malone* is a great example of consistent delivery of brand values in every aspect of the retail experience.

Jo Malone is clean-cut and modern, active and healthy, with fresh citrus, jasmine and pomegranate fragrances. It is an opportunity to pamper yourself or your loved one. The colours are understated cream in a, clean, uncluttered design, with a simple logo. Every item is consistent in its message and the product stays at the centre of the experience.

For example, when you buy a product at a *Jo Malone* store, your exquisite *Jo Malone* bag is given a tiny spray of *Jo Malone* fragrance before it is handed to you, so that the rest of your shopping trip is beautifully fragranced too, making you feel special.

As is clear from the above example, simplicity is often best in expressing clearly the values of your brand, even where there is a complex life philosophy underlying the brand and the business, as in the next example.

Best practice example: *John Lewis Partnership* is a British department store group with a unique business philosophy. As the name implies, it is a co-operative partnership of employees, rather than a listed company, with very strong social responsibility values and a long, well-earned reputation for quality and reliability.

On its web-site, the company explains, *"When John Spedan Lewis founded the Partnership, he set out how the business was to be run in our Constitution, a set of corporate values and principles which govern and guide our business. Our seven business principles purpose, power, profit, members, customers, business and relationships align perfectly with current thinking on corporate social responsibility. They set out how we see our responsibilities in terms of community investment, environmental protection, responsible sourcing and trading and workplace dignity, diversity and equality. Through the combined efforts of our Partners over the years, we have built a culture based on our principles, which ensures that corporate social responsibility issues are* embedded in the way we run the business. We believe that this unique Partnership culture, which makes sure we deal with our customers, suppliers and all stakeholders with integrity and respect, is at the heart of our commercial success."

These values permeate all of the language, messaging, slogans, advertising and working practices of the John Lewis Partnership. Customers immediately recognise this, trust it and enjoy the sense of becoming part of something that seems inherently good, a different world from the normal commercial enterprise. And they get super quality products at reasonable prices.

Clearly, whether a fresh young brand or one that has a long and rich history, the principles are the same – in everything the customer experiences, the brand values and lifestyle attributes your brand represents must be simply, clearly and consistently expressed.

Tools for projecting the brand values

Tool	Impact
Words	It is worth listing all of the words that most closely express the values of your brand. In the same way that "earth" and "green" have associations that will fit well with one brand, another might be better expressed as "space" and "time". Above all, ask what the emotional reaction of your customers will be to the words and then be very consistent in their use.
Colours and images	Like words, colours are laden with emotional and semantic associations and these must fit with your overall brand. Colours can also be fashionable, so beware you don't lock yourself into a passing colour trend, rather than a good expression of the brand.

	The Body Shop uses green a lot, *Virgin Atlantic* uses red, and both feel right. It is this fit that you seek to achieve, a colour that expresses the emotional and semantic attributes of your brand, the right level of energy and associations. When combined with simple images, you can quickly express your brand, even in the second or two someone glances across the mall at your store, and often that is all the time you have to attract attention.
Logos	It goes without saying that the logo must fit with the overall brand values, both visually and semantically, as this is the mental image that is recognised and becomes the symbol of everything the brand embodies. Even when this is a simple name, the name, its typeface and colours will themselves convey the essence of the brand. Consider *Jo Malone* and *Harley Davidson Motor Cycles* – both are names as logos, yet each encapsulates its brand perfectly in the way it is executed. Over time a brand can become simpler as customers adopt increasing amounts of the meaning. Take the *Nike* logo for example – the "swoosh" without the *Nike* name is just as recognisable as the *Nike* name itself. The *Harley Davidson* vision is: *"We fulfil dreams inspired by the many roads of the world by providing extraordinary motorcycles and customer experiences. We fuel the passion for freedom in our customers to express their own individuality."*
Packaging	Packaging must be consistent with the brand. As

	mentioned above, the *Jo Malone* packaging is a good example of best practice. It extends the colour, style and values of the brand and the bag becomes a walking advert as it is carried home by the customer, a badge of achievement that every woman will envy!
Environment	In a documentary, Tom Ford once described the process of assessing the customer experience by saying how he would sit outside a store in his car looking at the front of the store for several minutes to identify all of the obvious and more subtle brand signals to the consumer, then go inside and note the fragrance, the music, the colours, lines and overall impact of the product displays, store interior and the staff. He was emphasising the critical importance of the environmental cues in creating the customer experience and communicating the brand, *Desigual* lets the customer play a role in creating the environment and *Disney* spends as much time deciding on the fragrance to blow across an attraction in one of its theme parks as the colour it will be. Design the environment of the customer experience in all 5 senses with great care.
Relationships	Relationships are important in deepening and extending the brand. Brand managers realised very early on that films were great places to place products top share in the cachet of the film stars. This now works just as much in reverse, with particular brands appearing in films as short-hand for lifestyle statements. Remember someone using a computer in a film you have recently seen – 10:1 it was an *Apple.*

	Consciously design the network of relationships your brand must cultivate, as carefully as if you were planning your own social circle.
Causes and associations	In the same way as relationships are important, the causes you espouse as a brand and the organisations with which you associate, help to define you. *The Body Shop* supporting remote communities is a great example. The brand is seen as having a relevant social conscience.
Actions	And above all, no matter what you say or with whom you associate, make sure that every action is congruent with your brand. One action that contradicts the brand values can destroy years of brand building in one fell swoop.

Product

A common retail saying is "you are only as good as your product" and this is very true. All the clever branding, communication and experience-building in the world is for nothing if the product or service you deliver is disappointing. This will make your brand unsustainable and you will fail. The product is a core part of the customer experience, in its relevance, its quality and in its availability.

Best practice cases: *Whole Foods Stores* have their product at the centre of the brand – a wonderful, nourishing, rich variety of fresh goods to delight and surprise their customers. Imagine if, with this branding, a poor product assortment or bad quality product was offered – it would kill the brand.

The same applies to any other retail brand. Other best practice cases include *Jo Malone*, mentioned earlier. All of the fresh, modern and self-indulgent attributes of the brand are realised in the fragrances themselves – fresh and clean citrus, fruits and flowers.

Of course the main example used earlier, *Apple*, is another prime example of the importance of the products in driving brand success. The *Apple* brand would falter if its *Macs* were inferior or its *iPods* and *iPhones* did not work well, but each one is a testament to superb engineering, visionary design and superior usability, and so customers are consistently delighted. The brand consistently delivers on its promise.

So, as a consumer, what do I look for in my preferred products, consciously or sub-consciously? The first thing is that they must have *relevance*. What I mean by this is that the product delivers on the brand promise, consistently with the values of that brand promise, most basically in terms of doing the job for which it was designed, but also in being available in the format or model I need. A computer must not just meet my need and work well, it must deliver the computing experience promised by the brand – if the promise was "ease of use" then it must be easy to use, if the promise was "fits in your pocket", then it must fit, and so on. Failure to meet the brand promise at this most basic level will kill the brand. Full stop.

The second thing I look for in a product is *quality*. This is an extension of the relevance mentioned above, but is even more basic. A garment that comes apart after its first wash, no matter how brand-relevant, represents poor quality and poor value. The consumer will not come back to buy another one. In this sense the product experience is an extension of the customer experience.

Thirdly, I want *availability*. Availability means the product is on the shelf/rack/web-site when I want it, in the colour or size I require, so that I can buy it. Everything in my engagement with the brand has led up to this moment and poor availability destroys it. I might tolerate poor availability once or twice, but if it persists the brand loses value and I shop elsewhere.

Best practice case: *Zara*, the Spanish fashion chain, was mentioned in the first section of this book as having a remarkably responsive measurement system for "listening" to customers by monitoring daily what they buy by garment, by size, by colour, by store and then replenishing to reflect that pattern within the week. This is how it all comes full circle. *Zara's* system of listening also ensures it is able to deliver on the brand promise in terms of product relevance and product availability.

Tools for ensuring a great product

Focus	Question and the impact
Relevance	Is the product functionally and aesthetically consistent with the brand promise? Does it exist in the right colour, size and functional variants? The brand is reinforced and loyalty increased.
Quality	Does the product do what it is meant to do? Does it perform to an acceptable level of quality? Is it durable, etc? A hygiene factor – poor quality destroys the brand, good quality is expected.
Availability	Is the product on the shelf in the desired colours, sizes, formats and/or specifications when the customer wants it? The impacts are increased customer satisfaction, higher sales/fewer lost sales and increased customer loyalty.
Design values	Is the design simple, functional and effective? Is the design unique? More likely to appeal to a niche market (or set a trend!).
Fashionability	Does the product capture the mood of the time, of a generation or a community? More likely to be adopted as an icon that perpetuates sales – for example, the *iPod*, although supremely functional and simple in terms of pure product design, also became the badge of a generation.

The Customer Experience Process in summary

This completes the full cycle of the Customer Experience Process, from listening and planning to delivery, a constant cycle that must be run with rigour and discipline every day of the life of the retail brand if you are to sustainably deliver a truly differentiating customer experience.

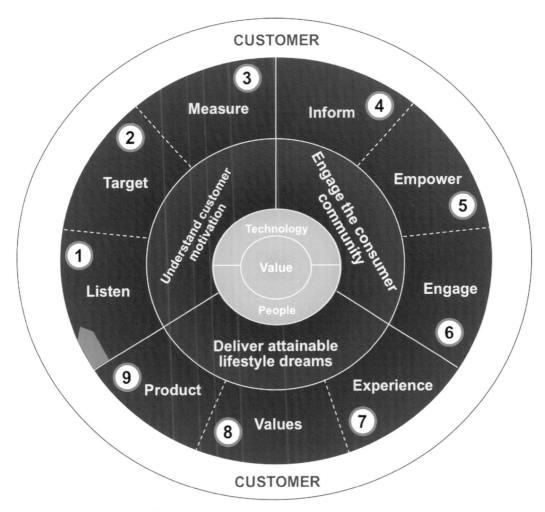

Diagram 23: Overview of the customer experience process

     To summarise, we have explored the three pillars of the process for delivering a great customer experience.

     This starts with truly understanding the consumer motivation, by listening, targeting the real needs of your chosen customers and measuring in an ongoing way how well you are reaching them. This is synchronising with the consumer.

The second pillar is engaging the consumer community, based on the insights gained from understanding their needs. You need to inform the customer of your brand, its values and promise, empower the consumer to act or achieve something value-added through your brand and engage them in a rich conversation or exchange to develop and deepen the engagement and its relevance for that consumer.

Finally, the third pillar, delivering attainable lifestyle dreams, where you deliver on the brand promise. This is done through creating a rich and relevant emotional experience, consistently living the values that your brand and your customer share and providing a great product or service.

We turn now to the two powerful enablers of the customer experience – your people and your IT systems.

Section 2: The 2 enablers of customer experience

In the store the interaction of the customer is often with a member of staff, either in the process of purchasing or at least at the cash register. A whole army of people a also busy behind the scenes, selecting products, creating adverts, designing promotions, executing the supply chain processes and so on. Every single one of these has a direct impact on the customer experience of the brand, especially the face-to-face experience in the store.

In today's multi-channel world, with increasing on-line purchases and with on-mobile services rapidly emerging, points of interaction with the customer on their journey are often interactions with technology. This technology must therefore be used to deliver a brand-relevant customer experience just as effectively, responsively and consistently as a trusted member of staff.

Diagram 24: The two enablers – people and technology

At the same time, technology is the enabler of much of our customer experience delivery process. It is smart technology tools that allow us to run modern loyalty systems and execute the analytics that enable deeper customer understanding. Smart supply chain systems ensure we can replenish stores in good time with the right assortment of products. And in the customer interaction on-line, on-kiosk and on-mobile, a synchronised set of processes are executed throughout the business to deliver the desired result. In short, it is impossible to run the modern retail business effectively without the right integrated systems and these are integral to delivering the differentiated customer experience.

In the following pages we will first explore in depth the ways in which you can best use your people in the customer experience process, before turning to a comprehensive exploration of the best approach to deploying the IT systems and services required to support the process.

The 1st enabler: People provide the connection

It has become a truism that your people are your face to the customer and so a critical differentiator within the customer experience.

The fact however is that most retailers employ large workforces that change rapidly, especially in the store, due to many temporary workers and frequently also low skills requirements. This means that, in reality, the most unreliable and difficult to manage area of your retail business is often the people and yet, as we shall see in this section, they are the face of the brand more than almost any other factor in the business.

Let me take the example of a shoe retail brand I advised some years ago in the UK. The brand was focused on the 18-25 year old market, a very fashion-savvy target market with a strong motivation to buy shoes, but with a relatively low disposable income. This brand had not been maintaining its rightful share of the market in spite of being named as the benchmark for fashion in the shoe sector and experiencing very high customer footfall in all of its stores.

I and my team surveyed a strong sample of the customers. There were two problems. One was the price point, something we had to address, but the other can be summed up in the statement of one 18-year-old customer, "The sales assistant reminds me of my Mum and I wouldn't ask my Mum to tell me what shoes are cool right now." Although the staff members were experienced and well-trained members of the team, in the experience of the customers, they were a blocker to buying the product, because they contradicted the brand – young, cool, fun, fashion shoes.

> **Best practice case:** A while ago I took some retailer customers of mine on a walkabout in London, visiting various stores to assess approaches to customer service. We were delighted when we went into the *Molton Brown* store.
>
> The store manager immediately welcomed us, was clearly passionate about the soaps, shampoos and aftershaves stocked. She was knowledgeable

about the company history and the product development and production processes and immediately engaged each one of us in an interactive process that led to sampling the products. This involved the store manager washing our hands with various of the soap products, an especially engaging experience.

Needless to say, we each bought something, enjoyed our visit tremendously and went home that night with a story for our partners. We have all been back since and I certainly continue to buy *Molton Brown* products as a direct result of that great customer experience.

Aligning your people with the customer experience you wish to deliver is something that must be consciously created. This needs careful planning and preparation, including programme of recruitment that create the alignment quite goal-directedly.

Next, you must organise your people (and other resources) for best effect, supported by the training and management practices that will deliver the customer experience and the business results consistently.

Leadership creates passion and imbuing your staff with a passion for the brand is critical – customers will feel it, whether indirectly through the care with which a product package is finished or directly via a shop assistant or call centre operator. Leadership is about clarity of vision, passion, engagement and communication, a sort of internal version of delivering a great customer experience – delivering a great team member experience.

And then you must measure and reward success, so that staff share in the success of your brand.

Creating alignment with the brand – planning

When you created your brand, you created its personality, making positive decisions about the values, attributes and ways that these could be experienced through the products and services you provide. It is this same brand personality that you want your staff to understand, be passionate about and indeed embody in their day-to-day work in your company, especially where this directly communicates the brand to consumers.

For this reason, it is useful to do a mapping exercise where you remind yourself of the brand values and attributes and the ideal customer experience down the left hand side of the page and then list the attributes of the ideal employee who would embody these, on the right.

Of course this is role specific, so a second layer of attributes must also be listed, relevant to the specific role – the competences required to do the job. Don't confuse the two. The first is the brand identity of the staff member, the second is the competence profile – the staff member needs both in order to do a great job for you, both projecting the brand values and doing a very competent job. This could look something like the following:

ROLE:	
Reports to:	**Direct reports:**
Brand values and attributes:	**Person's brand-aligned attributes:**
COMPETENCES	
Knowledge:	
Skills:	
Experience:	
Attributes:	

Organising and deploying your resources to deliver the brand

Of course roles don't exist in isolation, but as part of a complex network of roles in the organisation, working in synchronised fashion to deliver the brand and execute the business plan. For these reasons, the roles and people within them must be thought about in an integrated organisation, with due regard for what knowledge, information, skills, processes and behaviours will be needed in each part of the organisation to collectively deliver the right result.

So how do you organise your teams to ensure that the right customer experience is delivered consistently? There are a number of simple organisational measures for deploying and using your staff with precision, that go a long way to creating success:

- **Design your organisation structure from the customer back.** For example, if serving the customer personally in the store will best create the sales opportunities, then putting in place the right number and types of people in the store is critical, with a support organisation of product and service-knowledgeable people or tools backing them up directly or remotely and a service management structure to lead and orchestrate the effort.
- **Define roles in terms of the customer experience results.** For example, instead of describing a store manager role as intended "To manage the staff, resources and environment of the store to best effect to maximise sales", you may wish to shift the emphasis to "To deliver a memorable brand experience to every customer through the staff, resources and environment of the store, so that sales are maximised and sustained." This subtle difference communicates your expectations to your staff and also causes you to measure different things to assess success.
- **Describe explicitly what you expect from your staff.** Tell staff about the importance of brand, the customer experience and the supporting activities and don't just assume they already know. You will be repaid with precise efforts from committed and confident staff who know what is expected of them.

- **Train staff in the brand, its values and the customer experience requirements.** Training is too often regarded as a box-ticking exercise to meet administrative requirements, but giving your staff an in-depth understanding of the brand, its values and the customer experience requirements will make them passionate advocates for the brand, especially if they are also given an opportunity to create some of the messaging and approach relevant to their roles.

- **Create opportunities for synchronisation and communication between functions and teams**. A common complaint in most organisations is that people operate in silos, leading to fragmentation of effort and a breakdown of co-ordinated effort. Left unchecked, this can paralyse the organisation. In order to avoid this, you should consciously create multi-functional teams and the opportunities for people to meet, share ideas and collaborate across natural team boundaries.

- **Measure success in terms of customer outcomes.** We have become fixated on measuring success in our modern world and this tends to drive us towards easily quantifiable, but sometimes simplistic, measures. Sales must be tracked, but it is much more useful to know which sales were to new customers and which were returning customers. Even more interesting is to know what prompted the sale and how people perceived the brand before, during and after the sale. Be creative and find ways of sampling and measuring these qualitative aspects, so that you can guide your staff to even greater effectiveness.

- **Give frequent feedback to staff on how you are doing with customers, preferably using the customers' words.** Once you have qualitative feedback coming in, this is incredibly powerful in feeding back to staff, as it is not simply a manager expressing an opinion, but a real customer telling the staff member what is right or wrong. Creating opportunities for staff to attend customer focus groups is equally powerful.

Best practice examples: So, if you are to deliver the customer experience successfully, you must organise your people with care, train them well, deploy them with precision and then manage their performance supportively. This is what *Molton Brown* clearly does (see my earlier example) with its long-term staff and it is clearly what *Apple* does with its store staff, even though many of them are short term or temporary staff. They all share a passion, act confidently in showcasing the brand and therefore bring customers back again and again for a great customer experience.

Brand leadership through people

Good management is a basic requirement of business success, but good leadership is what makes the difference between being "just another retailer" and being a dynamic retail business that leads the way and conquers the competition, building a lasting brand that will delight customers over and over again.

A good leader is someone who has vision, can communicate that vision simply to others in a way that can be practically executed, someone who inspires, takes the time to listen to the team before setting the direction and leading the business to success, both directly and through empowering others.

Let's look at these attributes by turn:

- **Vision & inspiration.** Look back to the beginning of any great retail chain or store and you will find someone with a great retail vision, inspired by an idea. Replicating this in your leadership team and refreshing it is tough, especially as the company grows bigger, more complex and potentially more corporate. Devise actions and activities to recreate the vision and inspiration in the leaders and the business at regular intervals. I have found that "innovation showcase days" are a great tool for this.

- **Brand passion:** The same can be said for brand passion. The brand is an expression of the vision. Get your leaders to actively refresh and build the brand, with each other and with the people in the company.

- **Pragmatism.** But remember to always find very practical ways in which the vision and the brand can find expression in the hard light of day and in the lives of staff and customers.

- **Communication – listening, informing, teaching, giving feedback.** These must be done relentlessly and this will pay handsome dividends. People wither without communication and flourish where it is strong.

- **Setting direction.** Leadership is about showing people where to go. Clearly set the direction, articulate why and communicate deeply and frequently about this.

- **Leading the way.** Nothing destroys a brand faster than a leader contradicting the brand values. Take great care to "live the brand" as a leader and to take staff with you.

- **Inspiring and empowering others to lead.** There is always the danger with strong leaders that they want to keep control, but this places sharp limits on what you can achieve. Much better, having inspired others chosen for their skills, trained them and deployed them with precision, to empower them to create part of the brand too. This is the difference between having employees and having a team.

Best practice examples: Leadership can be flamboyantly inspirational, as in the case of Sir Richard Branson of *Virgin* fame, or it can be more understated, as in the case of Tom Ford, or richly demanding, as in the case of Steve Jobs of *Apple*, but ultimately leadership is about the same things – inspiring with vision, engendering brand passion and demonstrating practical ways of expressing this. It is rich in communication, leading people with clarity and direction, but also empowering them to become a valuable part of the creative brand process.

Measuring and rewarding staff for great customer responsiveness

It is of course critical to exercise control over your business and its results. This applies to the normal business measures of revenue growth and profitability, but equally to the success in delivering the differentiated customer experience, much of which is directly through your people.

Measuring success of peoples' performance means clear expectations should have been set, there must be a clear plan, with objectives and a mechanism for measuring. This closes the loop with the planning described above.

Measure success, recognise frequently and reward generously.

> **Best practice example:** The UK grocery chain *Tesco* operates a great scheme for allowing staff to share in success, both in their normal performance management system, but also in the opportunity for share ownership. The result is that many ordinary workers who have spent their working lives doing fairly basic, but critical jobs like till operation or shelf stacking, have been able to retire early with a great retirement nest egg, because their equity grew with the success of the company. This is just one example of how a retailer can share its success with its people by way of long-term reward.

We turn now to the second enabler, an increasingly important determinant of retail success in the increasingly multi-channel world – the role of IT.

The 2nd enabler: IT – technology provides the tools

It has become a truism that everything you do in retailing, or indeed in other industry sectors and your private life, depends in large part on the availability and effectiveness of IT systems, databases and smart tools for accessing these.

And yet it is true. Whether one is talking about the basic systems like telephones and cash registers, big enterprise processes like the supply chain, warehousing or loyalty programmes, or innovations in kiosk or on-line tools where you are directly interacting with your customers, every single one depends on the availability of synchronised systems, both inside and outside the boundaries of the company.

Fail to ensure the right quality and type of systems architecture is in place to support your business and you will fail, not only in your attempts to deliver a differentiated customer experience, but in effectively running the basic business itself. This is not to mention keeping up with the newest consumer trends and the technology innovations that must support these.

IT innovation best practice case: *Metro Group*, the German-headquartered grocery, department store and consumer electronics retail giant, recognised early on that it depended for its competitive effectiveness on embracing, supporting, exploring and sponsoring technologies and ideas of the future. For this reason it established the *Metro Future Store Initiative*, now in its second generation, where suppliers and IT companies can showcase and evolve the best of their new ideas and technologies in a live retail environment.

In order to deliver an effective customer experience, you must have the right IT in place. It must act as an integrated whole and it must be flexible and responsive enough to support your business as it evolves.

How do we do this?

I will outline the trends in IT and, more specifically, consumer and retail IT. This will be followed by a brief focus on the role of technology in supporting the customer experience in the context of the store, on-line and on-mobile, Business Intelligence and loyalty, as well as in the bigger enterprise IT architecture.

Consumer IT trends

The daily lives of consumers have evolved over the last thirty years from having very little IT intruding to having everything supported by digital tools.

To this extent teenagers spend huge amounts of time texting, talking on phones, gaming and on social networking sites. They cruise the internet for research for school or college, to investigate fashion, trends and music and to explore their extended world.

It would be a mistake to think that the ubiquity of technology is focused primarily on "young people", who are naturally more open to new tools and experiences. Technology has reached virtually every demographic group and lifestyle type. The business person is on their *Blackberry* and their partner is on a smart phone. Everyone is on-line and they are all using smart tools to access value-added information and functionality. All of this is made ever easier by the availability of broadband wireless networks in the home and on the high street.

People bank on-line, they submit their taxes, they book their holidays and buy insurance, research schools and colleges and explore the range of goods and services they may want to purchase and much more besides. And they do this every day, throughout the day.

These are the consumers who walk into your store and this is the ubiquitous technology they are constantly using – *Google, eBay, Amazon, last.fm*, on-line banking, government vehicle licensing sites, *Facebook, YouTube*, and so on.

Imagine their expectations of you and your retail business?

Generic IT trends

At the same time and in parallel, IT itself has been evolving into something altogether more powerful, more nimble and more accessible. Some of this has in fact driven some of the consumer IT trends mentioned above.

Until very recently, most IT systems existed mainly as stand-alone pieces of software, hard-wired in pretty fixed ways to all other applications in the environment. This meant that each piece of software had in-built expectations about how other applications in its environment would behave. Generally this was unchangeable without fundamentally reprogramming the application, as well as every other piece of software to which it was linked, so that a new set of expectations was hard-wired into this complex environment. This is what IT professionals are referring to when they talk about the problem of a "spaghetti" of fixed connections.

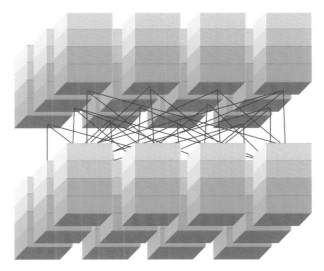

Diagram 25: A "spaghetti" of fixed connections between software programmes

In order to overcome the inflexibility of this arrangement, as well as to take away the enormous costs of maintaining and changing this environment as business needs change, technology innovators have developed a completely new approach to the way IT systems interact – this is called a "service oriented" approach.

In the service-oriented approach (IT professionals often refer to SOA or Service Oriented Architectures), software is broken up into reusable services and these are all connected into a single messaging system (also called a Message Bus). A new controlling piece of software is added to control the process of interaction between the services (a BPM or Business Process Manager). In this way, when there are changes to processes, it is only in the BPM that changes must be made, creating a cheaper, simpler and more flexible and responsive system.

In this approach, services can also be re-used wherever they are needed, rather than duplicated in different places. In this way a payment service could be used by several businesses and channels, rather than each business needing its own, even though payment may be featured differently in the various business processes.

Diagram 26: A Service Oriented Architecture (SOA) - allows application functionality or "services" to be re-used. Changes are made in the Business Process Manager (BPM)

In short, new technology has provided real-time, lower cost, flexible and responsive systems that are more open to interconnection within the enterprise and outside it. In this way someone else's software service can be used at a distance, along with your own in-house services – this is known as "Software as a Service" or SaaS.

Best practice case: *WalMart*, an innovator in the use of IT from its earliest days under Sam Walton, has converted all of its systems to a service oriented architecture and now benefits from increased flexibility, re-use of software services and lower IT support and maintenance costs, allowing it to concentrate more on the innovations that will deliver a differentiated customer experience or new value in the proposition it offers its customers.

Retail IT trends

Not surprisingly, the combination of the consumer IT trends and the generic IT trends described above has created a fantastic opportunity, but also a challenge, for retailers.

On the one hand we have consumers who are becoming more demanding, based on their experiences of great technology tools on-line at home. They are becoming more informed and have access to smart tools that can support them.

On the other hand we have IT systems in most retailers today that are still built in the old way, with a spaghetti-like plethora of fixed connections - slow, expensive and unresponsive. Even worse, the systems supporting different trading channels are generally completely separate – store, on-line, mobile, call centre, catalogue, etc., each in their own silo.

In order to respond to the consumer need for greater access to smart tools – to value added information and functionality – retailers want to provide a seamless brand experience across channels, supported by flexible and responsive systems that can evolve with the business. In short, they need to migrate to Service Oriented Architectures (SOA) and source some functionality from outside experts as Software as a Service (SaaS).

When I ask retailers what their business priorities are they always talk about delivering a great brand experience to customers, innovating in the stores, effectively managing their product categories and an efficient supply chain. When they talk about IT they have just two priorities:

- **How to overcome the inflexibility of legacy IT** and create a more joined-up multi-channel environment, with greater flexibility and lower cost
- **How to identify the right innovations to introduce at the interface with**

the customer by way of phone applications, on-line tools, kiosks in store, smart changing room devices, smart tills, digital media and so on.

Retailers are all trying to create responsive IT environments where they can respond to their customers in line with brand priorities and provide consumers with the tools to manage their own shopping experiences in line with their very individual needs.

So, what are the innovations are transforming customer experience?

IT supporting the customer experience

Store:

In the way IT is deployed and used:

- *Open architectures:* Retailers are replacing their in-store systems, such as the till systems (Point of Sale or PoS) with ones that are not hard-wired to each of the other systems. This creates more options for delivering functionality in different places simultaneously. For example, the till or cash register systems can be available on the till, on a hand-held device or on a kiosk, in each case interacting slightly differently with other systems. Needless to say, maintenance and support costs reduce dramatically in this more open environment, where changes must be made in just a few places, rather than in all applications when change is needed. These changes are taking place in the enterprise as a whole and not just in the store, but even in the closed environment of the store this adds huge value and enables retailers to be more responsive to customers.

- *Real-time:* It will surprise many people to learn that until recently and indeed still today in many retailers, the systems in place act locally for most of the day and then download all of the day's information from the store to headquarters and from headquarters to store, in an overnight "batch download" process. This means that it is impossible to respond to trends in shopping during the day from the centre, but only at store level, and then only with difficulty. A major development therefore in the systems available to support the store in terms of managing sales, loyalty transactions, inventory availability, etc. is that we have moved to near real-time data exchange between the store and remote locations like the headquarters. An altogether more responsive retailing becomes possible.

- *More flexible and responsive use of systems:* Along with the functional re-use that comes from a Service Oriented Architecture (SOA) in the store, increased flexibility also results from the increased responsiveness that can be delivered – instead of 12-18 months to introduce new functionality into the store, this can now be done in just days or weeks, depending on the complexity. Retailers can suddenly truly respond to current consumer trends in meaningful ways in the services they support in store with their IT. This frees the store from its recognisable model that has existed for hundreds of years and creates a whole lot of new options. Consider for example the *Nike* store that keeps almost no stock, but where you design your personalised trainers and pay for them, for pick-up or delivery. With traditional store systems this would simply not have been possible, yet many retailers still sit today with old, inflexible legacy systems supporting their stores. They are in danger of being unable to deliver the customer experience at the heart of their brands. The stockless store is a real option today.

- *Increased network reliability & bandwidth:* In order to communicate in real-time between the store and other locations you need to have a good network installed, with high levels of reliability and with enough bandwidth to cope with the increasing amount of data that must flow backwards and forwards between the store and other locations. Thankfully, networks have become ubiquitous and are increasingly available in fixed and wireless format in most developed countries and centres, though there are variations by country and region. For the most part, retailers are gradually moving to some greater degree of network dependence. This means that there is now the possibility of moving some of the computing power out of the store to a central location and operate a "thin client" or even "zero client" store – where local devices are dumb terminals relying on remote computer programmes. This brings powerful economies of IT operation and saves on hardware spend, but it also makes the retailer very network dependent. If the network goes down this can shut down the store. For this reason retailers are proceeding cautiously down this path to find the right balance between network dependence, resilience and cost.

- **Integrating systems, including multi-channel:** With the greater flexibility and openness of the various systems in store, real-time interaction with remote systems (including the ability to analyse shopping patterns), it has become possible to mix different systems' capabilities to create innovative points of service in the store. In this way digital media content can be delivered streamed into the store, visible on screens, on cash registers and kiosks and at points of promotion, which on-line internet access can be delivered in the store for both staff and customers. This is resulting in increasing innovation (see below) and increasingly satisfying ways of freeing the customer from the old-fashioned bank of cash registers as the primary point of interaction. Increasing mobility of devices is accelerating this process.

With all of these new capabilities in place at the level of store IT architecture and communications, it suddenly becomes possible to deploy all sorts of innovative devices and services in the store, mall or street.

Best practice case: The *Royal Ahold Group*, headquartered in the Netherlands, but operating internationally across Western and Eastern Europe, the Nordic region and the USA, runs a world class IT innovation team that works very closely with the business formats and operations teams to identify consumer and business needs that can potentially be addressed by IT innovations simply introduced into the store and multi-channel environment. Key though is that a very clearly defined *innovation discipline and piloting* *process* is employed to ensure that all innovations are properly evaluated and only those that truly add value, in the eyes of consumers and business operations staff, are retained and rolled out.

In this way, for example, a mobile phone payment system, using near field communication (NFC) technology, was developed and trialled amongst staff and a small group of customers, using a small store located at a railway station. This provided a wealth of insights that will guide the team in their further thinking and development of payment convenience for their customers, long after the trial ended.

Examples of specific innovations/new types of devices and services:

- **Point of Sale (PoS) becoming lean Point of Service:** As outlined above, the changing IT architectures in stores is allowing Point of Sale (PoS) systems to become more flexible points of service. At the same time, the transaction management functionality has become a commodity and can be re-used in other parts of the business. The other development taking place is that PoS hardware (tills or cash registers themselves) are becoming "thinner", that is, they have less and less local software and rely increasingly on the smart applications existing at the centre of the business, available to the "dumb client machine" remotely. In this way retailers are moving to what are called "thin client" stores and already exploring existing technology for delivering "zero client" stores, where there is no local software in the store. The results of these developments are twofold. In the first place the cost of store technology is dramatically falling, as is the cost of maintenance. In the second place it is rapidly becoming commercially viable to have a faster cycle of technology change in-store. Historically store systems have been refreshed every 8-10 years on average, whereas we expect to see more of a rolling refresh as costs reduce and more functionality is delivered virtually from remote data centres. We are in a period of revolutionary opportunity.

- **The self-service revolution:** In 2008 *Time Magazine* talked about the end of the age of customer service and the beginning of the age of self-service and this trend towards self-service is indeed accelerating. Whether you are in the grocery store in the USA or Europe using a self-service checkout machine or in one in Russia or China where self-payment stations are becoming common, this is becoming a key part of our lives everywhere and, in addition, much of what we used to rely on customer service representatives to do for us, we now do on-line as a self-service, not just in retailing, but in banking, utilities and government services too - increasingly supported by "virtual agents" as in the *Virtuoz* service used by *eBay* and *PayPal*. Expect this trend to increase.

- *Interactive devices and kiosks:* As consumers have become more used to accessing value-added information and functionality on-line and store IT architectures have become more accommodating, innovative IT companies and retailers have begun to experiment with a whole range of interactive in-store devices and kiosks.

  o One example of these is the varieties of "magic mirror" that have been created for use in fashion store changing rooms. How this works is that an RFID tag reader behind the mirror reads a smart tag in the garments that are brought into the changing room, with two results. One is that you instantly know what merchandise has gone into the changing room, a security benefit, but the more important result is that a projector behind the mirror is activated to project promotional images and text onto the mirror. This rear-projection makes the image appear to be floating in the surface of the mirror itself. Consumers love this experience, especially if the information provided adds value ("here's a blouse that will go with that pair of jeans") or if this is combined with an interactive button that allows the shopper to request the item being tried in another size or colour. A signal sent to a member of staff's hand-held device says, "A shopper in changing room no.6 needs a size 12 in item X – located on rack 5b". You can imagine the value-added possibilities.

  o Another innovation that has proven useful in high-advisory retail segments is the advisory kiosk. A good example is the make-up kiosk from *L'Oreal*. In the two varieties I have seen, the shopper can scan products (e.g. lipstick) or enter information on personal profile and preferences and the system will advise her on the best products to use, what combinations will work well, etc. The result is that the shopper gets exactly what she wants and needs, but probably buys more than if she were unassisted – a happy customer, a happy retailer and a happy supplier. *Metro Group* has found in its *Future Store Initiative* that kiosks that provide non-branded advice are even more successful because of the shopper perception of objectivity.

- **Staff mobility:** Retailers have always wanted to free in-store staff from the cash register to go out on the shop floor and sell, but this has been difficult, as all functionality supporting customer service activities was either on a PC or the cash register itself. However, with new IT architectures and some innovative hand-held devices on the market, retailers have begun to deploy mobile cash registers and customer service devices with staff in the store. A great example is *Apple's* use of mobile cash register devices (hand-held) in its stores, so that staff are not only advising at the "point of customer", but taking payment there too. Other functions include stock-taking for inventory management and the use of tablet devices to show stock not in-store - other colours of sofa in a furniture shop, for example.

- **Multi-channel in the store:** As customers have become more familiar with on-line tools that can also be used in the store – e.g. inventory search – retailers have begun to deploy these in-store for access to on-line facilities. This enables the shopper to meet his own need unassisted, but also for staff members who need to be as informed as the customers they serve.

Best practice cases: Good examples of on-line in store are *Borders USA* book stores and *Apple* stores facilities, but we have also seen experiments in the DIY sector and in other segments.

- **Customer mobility:** The modern smart phone has transformed the way consumers access and use information and digital tools. Each person now has the ability to build up their own portfolio of smart phone applications to support their daily needs, hobbies and interests. These apps are quickly and easily available, put powerful customised tools in the hands of the individual and can be used wherever the customer is. As a result, almost every major business is experimenting with, piloting or has rolled out a unique application. In the UK on-line grocer *Ocado* has a home shopping application on *iPhone*, *Waitrose* and *Tesco* have smart shopping assistants and a host of other retailers in different countries are using these kind of applications, as well as *Twitter* and other on-line tools on the phone to support their customers. This is the fastest growing area of innovation. In fact a retail CIO recently said to me he expected the customer mobile phone will be the only technology hardware retailers will need in 10 years time in order to trade in the store or on-line – a radical thought, but one which is surprisingly achievable. New innovations include *Layar,* a product from the Netherlands that combines augmented reality and GPS to deliver geo-tagged social media, location-relevant information and promotions

> **Best practice cases:** In the UK on-line grocer *Ocado* has a home shopping application on *iPhone*, *Waitrose* and *Tesco* have smart shopping assistants and a host of other retailers in different countries (e.g. *Borders USA*) are using these kinds of apps, as well as other on-line tools on the phone to support customers.

- **Digital media:** Another result of the digital revolution has been that digital content can be delivered anywhere and, because people today are so used to consuming programming and messages on television or computer screens, this is often seen by retailers as a desirable way of delivering information and promotions in the store. In my view, digital content is often badly delivered in-store, mainly because it is treated as yet another television screen where content can be delivered and consumed. The better uses of digital media are where these are used in unusual and innovative ways to catch attention, support promotions or deliver messages. The best example is one where two large plasma screens were placed in a clothing retailer, one on either side of an aisle leading to a swimwear promotion. When a shopper broke the beam of an infra-red sensor, this triggered the content – a crashing wave on the screen in the right, followed by a wonderful sunlit beach scene appearing on the left. It would take a very hardened shopper not to be energised by that and go on to take advantage of the swimwear promotion. Another very simple but effective use of digital media was one I saw in a grocery store promoting orange juice at the height of summer. Above a pyramid of orange juice cartons was a screen showing juice pouring into a frosted glass – simple and effective.

On-line:

The internet has grown from an interesting new channel 15 years ago to a critical route to the customer, comprising around 10% of the business of most retailers today. Not only this, but in high internet use countries like the USA, UK, Japan, Korea and Germany, this is growing at up to 60%+ per annum.

Whereas many of the early internet businesses of established retailers tried to simply sell the regular assortment of that retailer on-line on a similar model to the store-based business, most of the true innovators on-line were new entrants to the retail market – *Amazon, eBay*, etc.

This tradition continues, with much of the innovation coming from newer companies like *ASOS* and *Threadless* experimenting with new models or indeed the early innovators like *Amazon* extending theirs into new segments, with some innovations coming from established businesses like *Borders* looking for new ways to be effective in a changed world. Three key trends are:

- **Smart tools - personalised & interactive:** One of the most exciting developments on-line is the emergence of smart tools and apps for delivering personalisation and convenience. The first examples were in the music world (e.g. *last.fm*), but think today of a fashion site like *anthropologie.com*, where you can choose a swatch colour and immediately see everything in the range that matches that particular shade. Similarly, on other sites, there is image-matching software that allows you to mine the catalogues of several companies to find a style and colour of garment you want. *Nike* offers trainer design and personalisation in-store, on-line and on-mobile, as do *Adidas* and *Reebok*, amongst others. *ASOS* offers the chance to see catwalk video of a selected garment to help you judge its suitability. *Threadless* offers a T-shirt design kit. The list goes on and will continue to grow exponentially.

- **Social networking:** As social networking has grown into the phenomenon of the "noughties" it has attracted the interest of retailers and others wishing to leverage the viral power of these networks, both for gathering insights and for spreading marketing messages. In this way companies as diverse as UK catalogue retailer *Argos* (ran a competition on *Facebook*), Finnish fashion seller *Seppälä* (vote for who will appear in the adverts) and US bookseller *Borders* (genre clubs on-line, on-*Facebook,* on-*Twitter*, etc.) have experimented with and begun using these routes to the consumer exactly as traditional advertising has shown a dip in effectiveness. This is however a tough area to use effectively and I recommend that social networking be used as an extension of the customer experience, with a lot of emphasis on maintaining the integrity of the brand experience without appearing to be "…trying too hard to be cool". See the toolkit at the end of this chapter for some guidelines on leveraging social networking in delivering the customer experience.

- **Aggregators:** The other great innovation, which is both an opportunity and a threat for retailers, is the rise of the aggregators. At its simplest this is a group of people with a common need getting together to go directly to suppliers to assemble products or services for their members – a mother's group buying diapers directly from *Procter & Gamble* would be a good example. More commercially motivated services include the UK's *mysupermarket.com*, a site that allows you as consumer to compare your shopping list's prices across the major UK supermarkets to decide where you will get the best deal, and *mydeco.com*, a site that combines social networking, peer feedback, professional decorator services, smart tools and access to the catalogues of major DIY and furniture retail companies! Imagine if this were successfully offered in fashion or other segments, where there have been experiments, but no strong success stories yet. If you don't already know it, go to the *mydeco.com* site, explore its services, understand its model and then ask yourself two questions:

- ○ What will happen in my retail segment if an aggregator offers this sort of service?
- ○ Can I be the aggregator in my segment, offering this sort of service?

Best practice cases: Best practice cases in the on-line world today include retailers like *anthropologie.com, ASOS, Apple, Ocado, Argos, Topshop, Threadless* and *Ridemakerz*, in the regular retailing segments, in addition to earlier pioneers like *Amazon* and *eBay*, with *mysupermarket.com* and *mydeco.com* as some of the best of the aggregators. New best practices are emerging all of the time, so keep monitoring the internet for new players and ask why they are or are not successful – look at the brand experience they are offering their customers.

On-mobile:

As outlined above, the emergence of the smart phone has transformed the way people interact and the way in which they use value-added information and functionality wherever they are, deploying a personalised portfolio of smart applications that support them in meeting their needs and pursuing their interests. This is in its infancy, but growing at a rapid rate and I predict this will dominate much of the innovation thinking of the next few years and continue to transform the way we do everything in our lives from paying utility bills to accessing retail, banking and other services.

Because smart phones allow the shopper to access the on-line world, any on-line service is automatically also available on mobile phone.

Best practice cases: There are numerous great examples of really good smart phone applications, but five from different retail segments that give a good sense of the range available out there are: the grocery home shopping application from *Ocado* in the UK, a powerful tool for delivering convenience and utility; the "Find-it" product location smart phone applications from *Meijer* in the USA and similar one from *Albert Heijn* in the Netherlands, the fashion management tool from *H&M* launched in 2010, a well-rounded tool that offers personal fashion tips, viewing of fashion videos and searching by store, catalogue or other need, amongst other things, and the trainer customisation and ordering app from *Reebok*. Other trainer companies have similar apps on-line and on-mobile.

Business Intelligence:

As information processing has become more real-time, this has put increasing pressure on retailers to rapidly analyse masses of sales and supply data to accurately target consumers, reward loyalty, replenish stores with the right goods and order the right products for supply. This has also required multi-party access by retailers, their partners and their suppliers on shared IT platforms.

Business Intelligence applications themselves have become more sophisticated and able to analyse diverse data more easily and quickly than in the past. As outlined in the description of the history and role of loyalty (see Section 1), retailers have also become more sophisticated in selecting the right things to measure.

As a result, retailers today can customise reports for real-time, hourly, daily or weekly refresh as needed, as well as ad hoc analysis, using sophisticated tools either embedded in their ERP systems, or purchased from Business Intelligence systems suppliers that specialise in retailing (*SAS* and *MicroStrategy* are just two common examples).

Section 3: Above all…the value proposition

The reason your customers shop in your stores, whether in the mall or on-line, and return again and again is because of the value proposition you offer them. This is experienced as a "customer experience" which, as outlined in the earlier sections of this book, is most successful when it is the result of careful listening, targeting and delivery, but the outcome of the experience is that your customers have something they did not have before – a product, a service result or a great memory.

If they were shopping for a new coat, the experience is hopefully something they will remember, but the quality, durability and fashionability of the coat relative to the price paid are what will remain with your customer for weeks, months and even years beyond. This is the value proposition – not the experience on its own, but the product and price proposition that is at the heart of the experience, both in the store and in the months thereafter.

Diagram 27: The Value Proposition

Let's return briefly to the grids used in Section 1 to illustrate how you can understand your current positioning of your product and/or service and how these might be mapped to the emerging trends in customer experience itself, in consumers' increasing desire to be creative and in the increasing appetite for self-service, driven by technology tools that put knowledge and functionality in the hands of consumers. These same considerations are useful here – the first time we looked at them it was to ask who we are targeting and how, how this might evolve in future; now the question is how we can position our product and service to take best advantage of our chosen target audience's needs.

Remember the basic grid? This sets up the four things customers want in different degrees. It shows where multi-channel is in this (to the left of the broken line, but moving gradually to the right. It also shows where social networking intersects with the grid, where real world networking (e.g. meeting in the coffee shop) comprises the right-hand side of this space and on-line networking the left (e.g. on *Twitter* or *Facebook*).

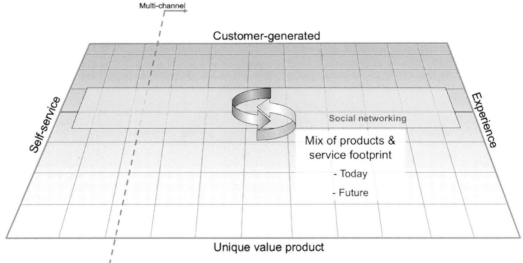

Diagram 28: A grid for understanding customer needs

What is the mix of needs and motivations within your customer base today and what are the trends in these in this target audience? You need to anticipate where your customers are going, but you can also lead them to new places with a great experience or offer.

The four broad areas of motivation are:

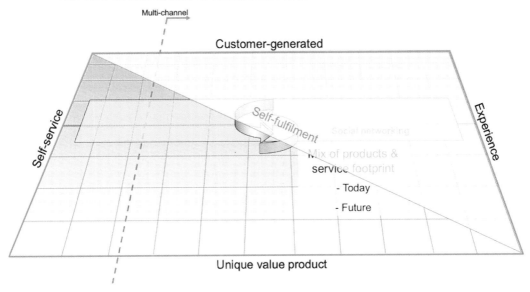

Diagram 29: The four broad areas of positioning with your target customers – self-fulfilment

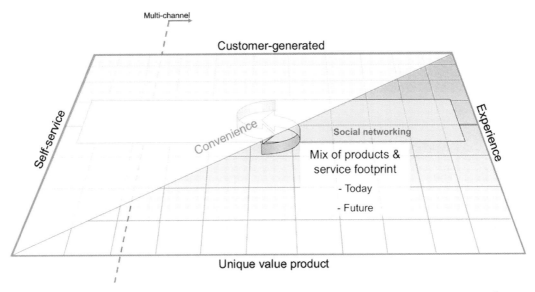

Diagram 30: The four broad areas of positioning with your target customers - convenience

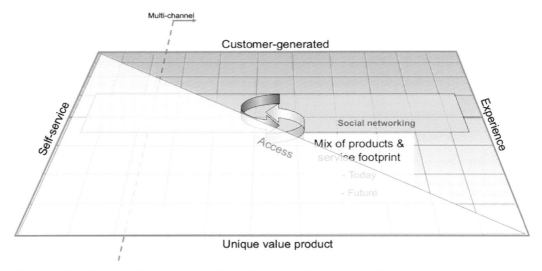

Diagram 31: The four broad areas of positioning with your target customers – access

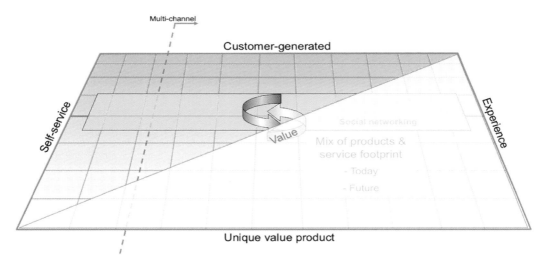

Diagram 32: The four broad areas of positioning with your target customers - value

In this way you are able to determine or estimate the extent to which your customers' needs will migrate in each of the three directions of self-service, customer generation and experience to determine your future footprint and the roadmap to getting there.

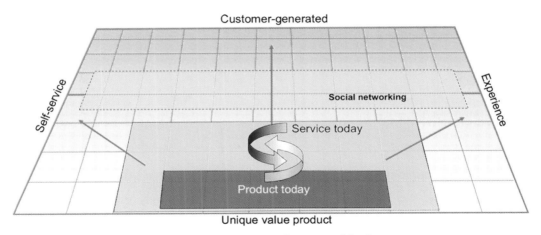

Diagram 33: Three trends we can exploit in our future positioning

This leads to a view of the services portfolio, the underlying processes and the tools that may be needed to support these.

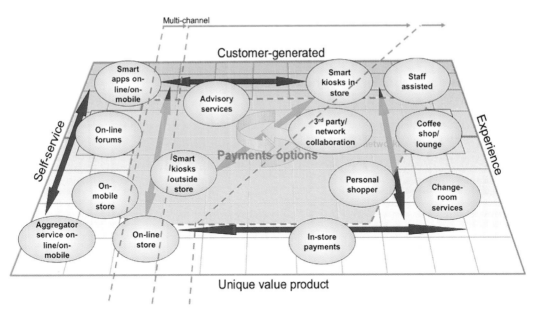

Diagram 34: A sample of processes, services and tools we need to consider across the grid

With that reminder, let's turn to a discussion of "the right product at the right price" – the core of the value proposition and the starting point for your discussions using the grids above.

Great products at the right price

Let's not forget the fundamentals of retailing. It is not by chance that the most successful retailers emphasise again and again - "product, product, product". Without the right product at the right price, all other measures you take are academic, so ensure that your teams are not so enamoured of the idea of "delivering the customer experience" that they forget that a great product at the right price is at the heart of that experience. Indeed it is often the physical embodiment of the entirety of the brand values invested in the experience and therefore the object of the whole exercise for the consumer. It is also the product that sits on the dressing table to remind them of your brand and its place in their life or the garment they wear as an integral part of their identity in landmark experiences in their life.

In addition, some of the most successful retailers in recent years have built their success on especially strong or unusual approaches to the product and price proposition. An especially successful example is Swedish headquartered, global fashion chain *H&M (Hennes & Mauritz).*

Best practice case: *H&M* has succeeded in bringing a new model to the fashion high street, a major achievement in a very crowded marketplace. The essence of the model is to bring designer fashion to ordinary high street shoppers as very affordable prices. To do so, they team up with top designers and celebrities like Madonna, to create ranges that are distinctive and desirable for consumers.

This taps into a fundamental need in their target market and demonstrates best practice in listening to and targeting the customer to deliver a differentiated customer experience. But the real beauty of the model is that the fashion is delivered to the high street at such affordable prices, putting aspirational designer and celebrity fashion within the reach of ordinary shoppers.

It is very rare for a retailer to come along and so fundamentally shape the market – *H&M* is fairly unique in this regard – but there are ways in which other retailers are using their products and pricing to deliver their value proposition to their target consumers every day in more regular, but equally powerful ways.

Best practice case: The UK's best known pharmacy chain *Alliance Boots*, also active across Europe, has for some years run its highly successful and admired *Advantage Card* loyalty programme. The *Alliance Boots* value proposition, as a pharmacy, is that of trusted advisor and provider of health and beauty products. Women are the primary target group and emotional and practical reward is the driving force. Its cosmetics counter is especially important to its shoppers.

By earning points on the *Advantage Card*, a number of rewards become available, from discounts through special offers, but the over-riding principle used is that the use of the *Advantage Card* should deliver a lasting emotional and practical reward to the shopper. In this way, a shopper will earn enough points to select a lipstick she might not otherwise buy, but this is made possible by the *Advantage Card* programme – and it will sit on her dressing table and remind her daily that *Alliance Boots* made this possible. This is a great example of the core value proposition being at the heart of the loyalty philosophy too.

In the example above, the whole idea of "the right product at the right price" is extended to encompass a much broader cross-section of the customer experience. The product is a set of desirable categories, products and services within the *Alliance Boots* brand proposition and the price is a complex function of the transactions in money and rewards points that define the relationship between the retailer and the shopper over time.

And these are just a couple of examples of best practice. Think of any of the great examples in earlier chapters or indeed your favourite retailer, whether a small, local business or a well-known, global brand, and you will see that successful delivery of a great customer experience in retail always includes "the right product at the right price". Think of *Apple, Il Palacio de Hierro, Ridemakerz,*

Desigual, Selfridges, Disney, Tesco and the others mentioned in this book, think of *H&M* and *Alliance Boots* discussed above, and all of them have a great value proposition in the product and price formula within their brand proposition, as played out in the differentiated customer experience they deliver.

Best practice case: In *Tesco*, primarily a food chain, the differentiating position taken very early on with regard to product and price was to effectively hold three ranges simultaneously. Whereas traditionally retailers choose to either lead on quality (with high price) or on price (generally with lower quality), *Tesco* developed the "good, better, best" approach to its assortment and pricing:

- *Good* is a good, basic, low-cost product that does the job, with no frills;
- *Better* is a middle of the range quality product with a slightly higher price;
- *Best* is the premium quality product at the highest price, best embodied in *Tesco* in the *Finest* range

It is worth noting that own label products exist in all three categories.

An important point to be made here is that there is no single "right answer". As you can see from the three very different best practice examples above, the exact way in which you present "the right product at the right price" is specific and integral to your business model and brand proposition.

Toolkit – three useful questions

Brand proposition	Remind yourself and your team what the core brand proposition is that embodies your brand in the eyes of the consumer.
Product	If they could engage with your products in any way they wanted to, what would your customers choose in your range? What is aspirational?

Price	What is the relationship of price to your products in the minds of the consumer? Is it a barrier to be overcome to achieve this aspirational product? Is it a surprisingly low price for the product or experience achieved?

Use these as the springboard for your discussion.

Conclusion: Run a successful retail business – deliver the customer experience successfully today and tomorrow

In the introduction I asked you to consider a Mediterranean market you might have visited. When visiting the market, you feel great because you have the warm sunshine on your cheek. The sky and the sea are bluer than you remember. Piles of brightly coloured fruit and lush vegetables invite you to touch, feel and explore. You can smell the fresh fertility of the earth and the produce. Each passageway suggests something exciting is just round that next corner.

The sights and sounds draw you in, along with the lazily milling crowd of other people similarly enjoying the market. You speak to people more easily as you drop your guard. You know that somewhere in the market there will be a vendor who is a bit of a character, inviting you to try the produce, engaging with you and others around you in light-hearted banter. You feel good. This is the life. If only…

You move on to the stalls selling honey and nuts, then leather goods – you breath in the rich smell of newly worked leather.

Whether it is this sort of experience that attracts you or another, depending on your personal preferences, what we all have in common is the desire to experience attainable dreams – the things that make up our aspirational lifestyle. We like the feelings these experiences evoke. We react emotionally with a sense of well-being. We begin to dream and plan how our lives might be transformed by engaging more deeply in the lifestyle evoked by these experiences. This could be in a very small way, as when a lemon-flavoured sweet briefly makes me think of the sweet lemons of Corsica, or in a more fundamental way, as when a great new outfit makes me feel as if I am living my aspirational dream.

A very powerful feature of the positive experiences is that they are best when shared with others, whether a partner or friends or, and this is a satisfying discovery, making new friends through the shared experience. This is how communities are formed – people organically grouping together and interacting based on shared experiences or interests that define a common, aspirational lifestyle. This is seen today also in the social networks that are constantly forming and reforming on-line.

And this social dimension is the heart of why people enjoy good shopping experiences. It is, I suggest, the single most important insight for any retailer, if they are to succeed. This is often strongest in younger shoppers who are exploring affiliations that will shape their lives and identities, and in women, who seem to have a stronger talent than men for creating and experiencing social communities in day-to-day life, though men are by no means exempt from this tendency.

This is what makes the customers of *Borders* USA book chain excited when they attend the book club readings with like-minded readers, to listen to their favourite author reading from his book. It is what makes them look forward to the *Twitter* messages and e-mail alerts of new developments in their chosen genre. It is what makes them visit the web-site and blogs to network with *Borders'* staff and other readers.

This is also why the customers of Mexican women's fashion chain *El Palacio de Hierro* flock to the stores and eagerly await the clever adverts, as the company has perfectly captured the spirit of "being a woman", transmitting a sense of belonging to a special group and using clever humour to highlight the unique strengths and challenges of being a woman. And so on.

There are many wonderful examples of great retailers getting it right – *Tesco, Apple, The Body Shop, Disney* and many more. I have explored a number of these during the book to illustrate the various principles and aspects of delivering a great customer experience.

This book is about how to deliver a great customer experience, so that you can create a successful retail business or transform an existing one. It has focused first on listening to customers, engaging them in a meaningful conversation and delivering the lifestyle experiences that make them come back again and again to spend their money in your store, whether a bricks and mortar, on-line or multi-channel store.

We then spent some time on the 2 key enablers of delivering a great customer experience – your people and technology. In order to establish and sustain the customer experiences that will define your business in the hearts and minds of your customers, you will need motivated people who live the business ideal, who identify with the customers' aspirations and who are passionate about what they do. You will also need very specific IT tools, as this creates the opportunity for engaging with the customer in multiple channels – an essential in today's world.

Finally, I discussed the value proposition – the importance of the right product at the right price in order to create sustainable value. This is the object of the experience, after all – to package and embody a value proposition for the customer and evolve this over time.

Diagram 35: The building blocks for sustainably delivering a great customer experience

…and in more detail in the diagram below.

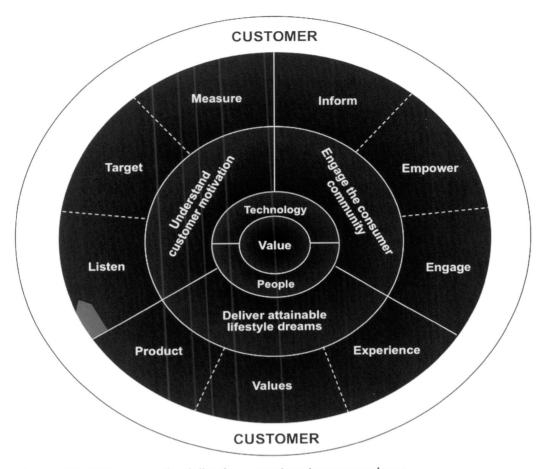

Diagram 36: All the levers for delivering a great customer experience

I trust you have enjoyed the book and the examples given, that you have learnt from it and, above all, that you have found it a useful and practical toolkit for transforming your retail performance through delivering a great customer experience.

I wish you well in your business.

Mark Dorgan
London
2010

-oOo-

Index of best practice cases and examples

INDEX